PENGU[illegible]

C[illegible]

GW00939308

Ranbir Vohra graduated from G[illegible] joined All India Radio as a pro[illegible] 1956 to 1959 he was seconded by the Government of India to study at Beijing University and, on his return, was put in charge of the Chinese Broadcasting Unit of the External Services of AIR. In 1964, Mr Vohra left the Indian government service to enter Harvard Graduate School where he received his M.A. and Ph.D. degrees in East Asian studies in 1965 and 1969. His primary area of concentration was modern China.

Dr Vohra taught at Harvard University from 1969 to 1971, and at the University of Calgary from 1971 to 1973, before moving to Trinity College, Hartford, Connecticut, where he is currently Charles A. Dana Professor of Political Science.

Ranbir Vohra has published widely on China and is the author of *Lao She and the Chinese Revolution*, Harvard East Asian Monograph, No.55 (Harvard University Press, 1974) and *China's Path to Modernization* (Prentice Hall, 1987). He has also edited *The Chinese Revolution: 1900 to 1950* (Houghton Mifflin Press, 1974).

PENGUIN BOOKS

CHINA

Ranbir Vohra graduated from Government College Lahore in 1946 and joined All India Radio as a programme officer in the same year. From 1956 to 1959 he was seconded by the Government of India to study at Peking University, and on his return was put in charge of the Chinese Broadcasting Unit of the External Services of AIR. In 1964 Mr Vohra left the Indian government service to enter Harvard Graduate School, where he received his MA and Ph.D. degrees in East Asian studies in 1965 and 1968. His primary area of concentration was modern China.

Dr Vohra taught at Harvard University from 1968 to 1971, and at the University of Calgary from 1971 to 1973, before moving to Trinity College, Hartford, Connecticut, where he is currently Charles A. Dana Professor of Political Science.

Ranbir Vohra has published extensively on China and is the author of *Lao She and the Chinese Revolution* (Harvard East Asian Monograph, No. 55 (Harvard University Press, 1974) and *China's Path to Modernization* (Prentice Hall, 1986). He has also edited *The Chinese Revolution, 1900 to 1950* (Houghton Mifflin, 1974).

Ranbir Vohra

CHINA

The Search for Social Justice and Democracy

PENGUIN BOOKS

Penguin Books (India) Ltd., 72-B Himalaya House, 23 Kasturba Gandhi Marg,
New Delhi 110001, India
Penguin Books Ltd., Harmondsworth, Middlesex, England
Viking Penguin USA Inc., 375 Hudson Street, New York, New York 10014, U.S.A.
Penguin Books Australia Ltd., Ringwood, Victoria, Australia
Penguin Books Canada Ltd., 2801 John Street, Markham, Ontario, Canada L3R 1 B4
Penguin Books (N.Z.) Ltd., 182-190 Wairau Road, Auckland 10, New Zealand

First Published by Penguin Books India 1990
Reprinted 1991

Typeset in Times Roman by Interpress Magazines Pvt. Ltd., New Delhi
Made and printed in India by Ananda Offset Private Ltd., Calcutta

To
Usha and N. N.

Contents

Preface

1989—the year China was to celebrate the fortieth anniversary of the founding of the People's Republic on 1 October—should have been a year of festivities. But the gunfire in Tiananmen Square that shattered the calm of Beijing on the fateful morning of 4 June not only cast a deep shadow over the Chinese nation, it focussed world attention on the Chinese crisis. People everywhere began to wonder what had gone wrong in the vast country that appeared to be doing so well under Deng Xiaoping.

Though the Tiananmen Square Massacre was directly linked to the student demonstrations, the student unrest was but a surface manifestation of the problems created by the economic and political reforms introduced by Deng Xiaoping. These problems, in turn, have roots that can be traced back to the economic and political developments under Mao Zedong. Therefore, for any satisfactory understanding of the current crisis, the predicament has to be examined in the larger historical context.

That is the aim of this book: to offer the general reader a broad overview of the complex but fascinating, and often bewildering, socio-political developments in modern China that culminated in the June '89 massacre. The last chapter is an exception; it deals with the Tiananmen Incident in great detail and is intended to provide a close look at the perplexing contradictions and tensions that influence the inner working of the Chinese political system.

In writing this book I have used many sources and am indebted to scholars, diplomats, and journalists who have published on China; for developments in the recent years I found the *Far Eastern Economic Review* and various People's Republic of China (PRC) publications to be particularly useful.

I would like to acknowledge my deepest gratitude to Professors Fred Drake and Robert Battis for their careful reading of the manuscript and their valuable suggestions for improving it. One realizes the true value of friends when one is working under a time constraint, as I was.

The greatest help was provided by my wife, Meena, who never lost her patience with me or enthusiasm for the project.

My thanks also to Trinity College for giving me sabbatical leave, without which the book would never have been completed before the 31 December deadline.

This brings me to David Davidar, the Editor of Penguin (India) who first came up with the idea that the China crisis called for a book that would provide the general reader an integrated view of the social, economic and political developments in that country. I agreed with him heartily and accepted his invitation to undertake the difficult, but personally satisfying, task.

December 1989 *Ranbir Vohra*
West Hartford
Connecticut

Introduction: 'Tiananmen Incident' 1989

For very different reasons, 1989 will stand out as the most momentous year in the history of European and Chinese communism. It was a year which witnessed a massive and dramatic outpouring of popular discontent against authoritarian communist regimes. Though the nations of the Eastern bloc cannot be treated as a single case, 'people power' in the communist states of Europe did produce a common result: with a few exceptions, regime after regime was forced to jettison the totalitarian communist order for a more liberal, pluralist 'democratic' system. Even if Marxism–Leninism survives the onslaught, what remains will be in a drastically altered form. Regardless of the final outcome, the faith of the believers in Marxism has been grievously undermined. In contrast to developments in Europe, China presented a totally different scenario. In the spring of 1989, a 'democracy movement' unfolded in China, too. But on the infamous morning of 4 June, barely four months before the country was to celebrate the fortieth anniversary of the founding of the People's Republic, a shocked world watched with horror (thanks to the international television networks) as tanks, armoured vehicles, and soldiers with automatic weapons, moved into Tiananmen Square in Beijing against unarmed students and citizens demonstrating for reform. The democracy movement was ruthlessly suppressed and the voice of dissidence stilled for the immediate future.

The Chinese leaders justified their action by saying that they had saved the nation from a rebellion that would have overthrown the state and the party. The outside world called it a massacre of non-violent innocents.

The Beijing incident raises many questions. Were the demonstrators rebels, or were they patriots who merely wanted to bring their grievances to the notice of the regime? Were the student demands so incompatible with the regime's goals that the regime had no option but to crush them? Did the students have the support of the masses? If not, why was the army called in to do the work of the police? Had the students been used as pawns in an intra-factional struggle for power within the party? Had the party lost its legitimacy and tried to maintain itself by force? What is the future of democracy in China?

To answer these questions, the 'Tiananmen Square Massacre' must be placed in the broader historical context of the Chinese Revolution. It is only through an examination of the tortuous path China has traversed in its search for modernization that we can gain a better understanding of the nature of the Chinese political system and the unresolved issues that face the Chinese leaders.

1

The Making of the Chinese Revolution, 1850–1949

Change, associated with modernization, has come slowly to countries like China and India that have strong, well-defined cultural traditions. In China, the hold of Confucian socio-political culture was so deeply entrenched and omnipotent, that its modification could only be achieved through revolutionary upheavals. Thus, the 1911 Republican Revolution, the 1928 Nationalist Revolution and the 1949 Communist Revolution can be looked upon as a single continuing process of modernization that may be identified as: 'the Chinese Revolution'. Indeed, this revolution can by no means be considered to have come to an end even in 1949. The spasmodic upheavals that have marked politics in the People's Republic of China since its inception reveal how China is still grappling with the problems of adjusting inherited values and institutions to the demands of modernity and development. The student crisis in 1989, leading to the Tiananmen Square Massacre, was just the last in the series of crises that have distinguished Chinese politics under the communist regime.

Modern Chinese history can be said to begin around AD 1800, when Western nations tried diplomacy to get China to lift its constraints on foreign trade which was restricted to the single port of Canton, and to accept Western-style diplomatic intercourse. (The Chinese, as will be discussed below, had no notion of the 'equality of nations'.) Having failed in this endeavour, Britain, representing the interests of the West, used its military power to 'open' China.

The Opium Wars of 1840 and 1860, regardless of their immediate causes, came to have a profound impact on the future political development of China. In many ways these wars were inevitable because the expansive and self-confident Western countries that had experienced the Industrial Revolution were clamouring for raw materials and markets and could not tolerate China's self-imposed isolation, or its attitude of superiority. The West that defeated China represented a new, powerful historical force that was in the process of dragging non-Western societies into a West-dominated world economic and political order. By the end of the nineteenth century, capitalist Europe had become the heart of a capitalist world economy in which non-Western states, China included, were incorporated as peripheral supporting units, either by direct or indirect political domination. Although, Japan, which had successfully Westernized and modernized by the late nineteenth century, joined the West in exploiting China, it had yet a long way to go before it could change the picture of a Western-dominated global order.

For a hundred years following the First Opium War, Western foreign powers, joined by Japan, repeatedly humiliated China and threatened its territorial integrity. It was under these conditions that the Chinese, desirous of strengthening the state and increasingly aware of the need to adjust to the unavoidable Western norms, began to 'modernize' by borrowing Western ideas, practices and institutions.

However, before the Chinese could turn to the West for the new knowledge of state management, they had to discard the view that the traditional Chinese culture provided the only basis of true civilization and had to accept the notion that Western civilization was in some ways superior. Ingrained habits of thought made this transition difficult, and for several decades after the First Opium War China continued to ignore the need for a better understanding of the West. Even after the weight of Confucianism was lifted—indeed, even after Confucianism was officially discarded and China went through a series of revolutionary upheavals—traditional values and practices continued to influence the process of modernization.

Inheritors of a rich, ancient civilization which had over 4,000 years of historical continuity, the Chinese were deeply imbued with the belief that they were a superior people who lived in the self-sufficient and self-contained, civilized heartland of the world, 'the Middle Kingdom'.* As a corollary, they

* Zhongguo, the Chinese name for their country which can be translated as the middle or the central kingdom.

also believed that all peoples outside the Middle Kingdom were barbarians, lacking both civilization and material goods. Therefore, while the Chinese had nothing to gain through any intercourse with the outside world, the barbarians (whether the 'long-nosed', 'red-faced' barbarians from the West or the 'dwarf' barbarians from Japan) of necessity came from long distances seeking China's civilization and her goods. According to the Chinese worldview the emperor of China, 'the Son of Heaven', was the benign ruler of all mankind. The notion that other nations were 'equal' to the Middle Kingdom could not arise. For over 200 years Western traders, too, supported China's self image of undisputed supremacy by working peacefully within the Chinese system. As a consequence, the self-assured Chinese scholar-bureaucrats remained woefully ignorant of the world outside China's tributary states, especially the countries in the West.

The nineteenth century changed all that. The Opium Wars and the 'unequal' treaties that followed humiliated China and reduced it to a third-rate power. If China had any pride left, it was destroyed in the 1894–95 war with Japan, when the 'dwarf' barbarians dealt China a crushing psychological blow by soundly defeating the Chinese forces, both on land and sea. The cost of the war depleted China's financial reserves, and the indemnity demanded by Japan forced China to take huge foreign loans secured by custom revenues—China's only dependable source of revenue. Then, from 1895 onwards, every crisis between China and the foreign powers only added to China's foreign debt, a financial burden that the nation would only escape with the establishment of the Communist Government in 1949.

Immediately following the Sino-Japanese War, Western powers, fearful that the Manchu dynasty (1644–1912) was on the verge of collapse, hastily carved China into 'spheres of influence' and forced the Beijing government to grant them special rights (to build railroads, open mines, etc.) within their spheres. This made a mockery of the Chinese sovereignty, which had also been eroded by foreign occupation of Chinese territory, foreign acquisition of leaseholds of ports and lands adjacent to ports, and foreign dismantling of the Chinese tributary order. Russia had occupied lands north of the Amur river and east of the Ussuri river in north-eastern China; Japan had absorbed the Ryukyus and Taiwan, Britain had taken Hong Kong; and Portugal had legalized its hold over Macao; the Germans had gained leased territory in Shandong, the Russians in Liaodong peninsula, the French in the south at Guangzhou Bay, the British in Shandong and in the area adjacent to Kowloon (Hong Kong); France took over China's tributary states of Indo-China, the British seized Burma, and the Japanese removed Korea from the Chinese orbit.

It is conceivable that China could have been turned into an outright colony, but mutual jealousy among the Western powers prevented that from happening. This meant that unlike India, where the British (for reasons good, bad or indifferent) became responsible for that country's modernization, China had to struggle to find its own response to the challenge posed by the West. The efforts of the Chinese Reformers and revolutionaries, searching for a path to transform China into a modern state, were both handicapped and helped by China's great Confucian tradition.

The Confucian Legacy

Imperial Confucianism, a combination of various philosophic and political ideas that had evolved over a period of many centuries before the Christian era, was the foundation on which the Chinese centralized monarchical system came to be structured (c. 200 BC). The Confucian ideology that held the system together was holistic and embraced the totality of a human being's social connections. It defined the relationships between mankind and the universe, society and the family unit, the family and the individual, and between culture and politics. The ideology was secular (disdaining interest in questions of 'afterlife') and provided an ethical, rather than a legal, socio-political framework in which the emperor, the Son of Heaven, occupied the pivotal role.

In their search for an alternative political system in the twentieth century, many Chinese intellectuals finally opted for Marxism because, among other reasons, there was a comforting affinity between certain aspects of Marxism and Confucianism: both were holistic, and Mao Zedong, as the new 'emperor' of China, even made leadership a function of ethics.

Society and the Law

Confucian society was family-centred, hierarchic and patriarchal. Since the highest goals of Confucianism were social order and harmony, the ideology emphasized proper behaviour between the basic 'three relationships': husband–wife, father–son, ruler–subject. These relationships were unequal (the husband, father and ruler being superior) and demanded that the inferior offer unquestioning obedience and loyalty to the superior; theoretically, the superior in return was supposed to exercise benign paternalism and look after the moral and physical welfare of the inferior. There was no place for Western-style individualism in this pattern of social intercourse in which the junior/inferior was always denied the power, status and precedence accorded by society and law to the elder/superior.

In an ideal situation, if everyone recognized his or her place in society and acted according to one's status, there would be no conflict, and harmony would prevail. When conflict did arise, the expectation was that it would be dealt with within the collective unit (the family, the village, the merchant guild, and so on) by arbitration and moral suasion.

The state legal system, which was primarily administrative and penal, came into operation only when the local group, or collective, failed to deal with a crime. Law was then used with excessive severity, as an instrument of state to instil fear into the hearts of the evil-doers and set an example, not to distribute 'justice'. The social unit to which a culprit belonged was held jointly responsible for the crime, because it had failed in its duty to instil proper Confucian values of loyalty, obedience and harmony. Since the ideology stressed duties and obligations within a hierarchical social system and allowed no place for individual or civil rights, the concept of a transcendent law never developed; for example, a father who had killed his son in anger would receive a light punishment (he had the right to admonish his child), whereas a son who had merely injured his father would be executed (the son had broken a cardinal rule of social interaction by raising his hand against his parent). As a consequence, civil law had a stunted development and China did not evolve an independent judiciary or the science of jurisprudence.

Even today, individualism has no place in communist China, and the legal system is still weak, used more as an instrument of state than as a device to protect the private citizen.

Government

The Confucian notion that China could be ruled over by only one monarch, the Son of Heaven, was so deeply entrenched in the psyche of the Chinese people that it buttressed the *unity* of the country and enabled a *centralized* imperial state to last for over two thousand years, from 221 BC to AD 1912. The idea, translated into modern terms, that there can only be one legitimate government for all China, exists even today; unlike India where the central government is perpetually trying to keep regional 'independence' movements from destroying the political unity of the country, the Chinese, under the communist government in Beijing and those under the republican government in Taiwan, take it for granted that one day they will definitely be reunited.*

Apart from this 'modern' feature of the ideal of unity, the Chinese political system had several other elements that appear very similar to those found in modernized societies. For example, the Chinese government was run by a bureaucracy recruited through an examination system, and the institutions of government included central ministries (such as Revenue, War, Public Works, Punishments, and Civil Affairs), provincial governments under governors, and district administrations headed by district magistrates.

Though it had served its purpose admirably by sustaining stability and unity in traditional China, the Chinese system was faulty and it became an obstacle in China's path to modernization. The biggest flaw, that will become evident from the following discussion, lay in the incompleteness of the centralized imperial institutions of the emperor and the bureaucracy.

Confucianism exalted the ruler's position above that of all mankind by declaring him the 'Son of Heaven', an intermediary between Heaven and

* China's problems in Tibet are an exception and a result of the fact that the Tibetan people are historically, geographically, ethnically, and culturally quite different and distinct from the Chinese and that Tibet was not an 'integral' part of China till the communist takeover.

Earth. We have already noted what influence this had on shaping China's worldview. Within China, people viewed the emperor as the fountainhead of Chinese civilization, the acme of Confucian perfection, the protector of Confucian ideology, and the 'father' of the people. As such, he was 'the basis of the State', over which he had absolute power.

People sincerely believed that the august person of the Son of Heaven radiated celestial majesty. Ordinary people could not look at him, and when his entourage moved down a road, it was cleared of the populace. Even high ministers had to kneel in the emperor's presence and keep their eyes low for the entire duration of an audience, which might last for hours. After 1380, when the office of 'prime minister' was abolished, the bureaucracy had become headless and lost its collegial deliberative, policy-making powers and, consequently, its value as a counterbalance to the autocratic authority of the emperor. While a prime minister could offer unsolicited advice, and even go so far as to criticize the emperor's policies, no minister now could dare do so. The emperor alone made all the final decisions.

Since neither the emperor's policies, nor the single imperial ideology of Confucianism could be challenged, the system allowed no place for the development of a 'loyal opposition'. Any person who dared to question imperial policies or imperial ideology was automatically denounced as a traitor, and dealt with accordingly.

One of the emperor's functions was to instruct the people to become better Confucian citizens. He was the Great Teacher at the apex of society; he personally examined the scholars who had passed all the requisite civil service examinations and were qualified for appointment to the imperial bureaucracy. Theoretically, the emperor was also supposed to 'educate' the common folk, but in reality, the emperor's instruction at that level amounted to no more than repeated warnings to the citizenry that they must be docile and submissive, respect authority, keep harmony within their families, obey the laws, and pay their taxes.

At a more mundane level, the emperor was the commander-in-chief of the armed forces and the chief administrator and law-giver. By the time of the Qing (the dynastic name of the Manchu regime) dynasty, the state had become highly authoritarian, the rulers despots. If this imperial power had been true Westen-style despotism the emperor could have mobilized the country to accept change and modernization. But this was not the case. The doctrine of 'the Mandate of Heaven' legitimized the emperor's rule, which implied that the ruler had no absolute right to rule; if he failed to live up to his Confucian duties of ensuring the people's welfare and maintaining social harmony, the mandate could be withdrawn. This doctrine justified popular rebellion against a bad ruler and legitimized the change of dynasty. So the prudent ruler, however omnipotent in theory and despotic in practice, could not afford to introduce changes that would disturb the traditional pattern of social relationships. Indeed, he needed to nurture his Confucian image carefully, because only adherence to the Confucian codes of behaviour could guarantee the people's loyalty to the system that was so deeply embedded in the ideology.

The Qing rulers, therefore, were understandably loath to encourage moves towards modernization, which necessitated a restructuring of the state. In any case, even if the government had been willing to introduce reforms, its success would depend on awareness of the ruling elite (the gentry-bureaucrat class that formed the elite is discussed below) for the need for reform. Without the ruling elite's support, the government's endeavours were bound to fail. Moreover, since the creation of such an awareness required a departure from the traditional educational system, based wholly on Confucian texts, in order to include Western knowledge, such a change would have undermined the foundation of the traditional Confucian imperial system.

This is exactly what happened in the late nineteenth and early twentieth centuries. When the 'spheres of influence' were established in 1898, the Guangxu emperor (who ruled from 1875–1908), alarmed at the prospect of China being wiped out as a political entity and inspired by some young reform-minded scholars to save the nation by Westernizing it, issued 200 decrees and edicts in 103 days 'ordering' the reorganization of China's administrative, military, financial, educational, and legal institutions. 'The Hundred Days' Reform' was a fiasco. The decrees alienated and threatened all the elites (scholars, bureaucrats, the military, and the Manchus) because they had a vested interest in the traditional order, which the reforms were certain to undermine. The result was that the emperor was put under house arrest by the empress dowager, Cixi; the Reformers were executed, or escaped to Japan.

In 1900, the anti-foreign, conservative Cixi diverted a local peasant rebellion (the Boxer Rebellion) from attacking the government to attacking Westerners and besieging their legations. The story is rather complicated, but need not be repeated here; it is suffice to say that the result was that foreign troops, representing eight nations, entered Beijing, broke the siege and raped the capital. China had to accept another crippling settlement, under which she not only had to pay 450,000,000 ounces of silver as indemnity, but had to execute and punish several high officials for their anti-foreign activities, as well as to allow foreign troops to be posted on Chinese territory.

Chastened by the experience, a much wiser Cixi herself became a proponent of modernization. In 1905, she terminated the imperial civil service examinations and introduced other reforms to prepare the country for a constitutional monarchy. The new, Westernized educational system instilled a sense of nationalism among the intellectuals. A modern attitude of loyalty to the 'nation state' replaced the old loyalty to the dynasty and the emperor, and the imperial institution became redundant.

In less than three years, on 10 October 1911, a revolutionary movement rose which swept the Chinese imperial institution off the stage of history by 1912, and a Republic was proclaimed.

The Gentry

In traditional China, the unity of the state, symbolized by the emperor, was ensured by the landlord-literati class (referred to by Western scholars as 'the Gentry') which acted as an intermediary between the official bureaucracy and the peasant masses. Trained in the Confucian classics, the gentry were the products of the civil examination system; those who passed all the three levels of examinations became bureaucrats, while the rest entered the ranks of the local gentry. In return for certain privileges, the government expected the gentry to perform specific unpaid functions (to supervise local public works, public welfare, and education; arbitrate disputes, etc.) that paralleled the work of the government. Without the million-plus gentry, the small bureaucracy of about 40,000 officials in a country with a population of over 400,000,000 would have proven ineffective in running the state.

The gentry thus provided 'unity' to the state, acting as a sort of 'Confucian cement' between the rulers and the ruled. But by the same token, they contributed to the absence of true social 'integration', a characteristic demanded by a modernizing country. A dynasty that lost the support of the gentry invariably collapsed.

The bureaucracy maintained strong links with the gentry; it rose out of the gentry, and when an official retired, he went back to his home district and became a part of the local gentry. The bureaucracy-gentry combination produced a tyrannical control system that allowed for the exploitation of the peasantry. Indeed, the government itself encouraged corruption by allowing the underpaid officials to 'officially' supplement their salaries by squeezing the peasants. Since this could best be done by conniving with the gentry, the gentry could not be denied a similar right. As a result, the Chinese allowed the evolution of massive corruption at all levels. 'Corruption,' as Professor John King Fairbank has noted, was 'built into the Chinese polity.'

It was the communists who finally brought modern-style unity to China by liquidating the landlord-gentry class and establishing direct links between the peasantry and the government. But even the communists have not been able to rid the system of 'bureaucratism' and the nepotism and corruption that accompany it. The over-concentration of authority in the hands of the emperor, a superficial bureaucracy, and an absence of a loyal opposition, contributed to bureaucratism. Contemporary Chinese government suffers from similar shortcomings.

The Republican Era, 1912–49

The 1911 revolution replaced the imperial dynastic government with a constitutional democratic republic. This was, no doubt, a radical development, but old habits of thought and social relations cannot be eradicated overnight, and the Revolutionaries had had no time to inculcate Western values of 'democracy' among the people. Indeed, it is debatable whether the new leaders fully understood the Western democratic ideal.

In any case, the revolution had been incomplete. The Manchu dynasty was overthrown, not by a cohesive, well-defined group of Revolutionaries, but by the Han* elites as a whole; even frustrated Han Reformers, alienated by Manchu ineptitude, had joined the Han Revolutionaries in their view that the Manchus had to go.

However, abolition of the dynastic system had in no way solved China's problems, it only added to them. On the one hand, the new rulers inherited an empty treasury and all the issues related to the aggressive foreign presence, while on the other, they had yet to legitimize the republic on the basis of popular sovereignty (the Mandate of Heaven no longer applied) and reunite the country (no longer held together by Confucian ideology) on 'modern' lines. This was easier said than done.

The New Legitimacy: Popular Mandate?

Although many Chinese scholars contributed to the intellectual climate that fostered revolutionary thinking, the writings of the Reformer Liang Qichao (1873–1929) and the Revolutionary Sun Yat-Sen (1866–1925) are particularly important.

Liang had been involved with the 'Hundred Days Reform', but when that idealistic but naive attempt to reshape China by fiat ended in failure, he saved his life by fleeing to Japan. During his exile in Japan, Liang captivated the imagination of Chinese youth and stimulated their patriotic passions with his writings, covering a host of subjects that explored Western thought, from history and politics, to economics, literature, and theology.

Initially Liang was entranced by the democratic principle of individual rights. As a good Confucian, however, he found it impossible to accept the notion that individual rights could be in conflict with the state. He elaborated the theory that an individual's best interests were always in harmony with the best interests of the collective, and that popular par-

---

* The Han people, the 'real' Chinese, formed the majority of the Chinese population, somewhere around eighty-five per cent, as against the Manchus, who constituted about two per cent, and were looked upon as 'barbarians' from Manchuria.

ticipation in government was, therefore, bound to strengthen the state. Liang's advocacy of democratic liberal principles was not intended to promote Western-style 'individual freedom under law', but to harness the energy of each individual to energize the collective.

Years later, having considered the issue in greater depth, a more mature Liang came to the conclusion that conditions in China were not ripe for even this limited version of democracy. The backward, ill-educated, undisciplined people of China needed an enlightened despot to simultaneously control them and tutor them towards a higher civic consciousness. The notion of a Confucian emperor who 'enlightened the people with education', had returned in modern garb.

Liang had wavered between support for a constitutional monarchy and for a republic. Sun Yat-Sen, on the other hand was an out-and-out revolutionary who had no reservations in pressing for the overthrow of the dynastic order and the establishment of a republic. As an anti-Manchu revolutionary with a price on his head, Sun could only operate from outside China; he, too, had made Japan his headquarters.

Sun's theory of revolution was based on 'three principles': (1) nationalism, which before 1911 meant anti-Manchuism, and later 'anti-foreignism' and anti-provincialism; (2) democracy (discussed in some detail below); and (3) 'people's livelihood', which implied a kind of economic socialism. Sun championed republicanism because it was the most advanced political system in the West; once introduced into China, it was bound to make China as strong and wealthy as the Western nations. Sun's belief was shared by even his opponents. However, Sun, even more than Liang, had no profound understanding of either republicanism or the principles that guided Western democracies. As if an answer to Liang's contention that the Chinese needed a long-term education in citizenship before democracy could work, Sun put forward a three-stage programme: military government for three years, followed by six years of political tutelage (when the government would teach the people democracy), leading to the last stage when the country would have an elected parliament and president. As far as the Western value of 'individual liberty' was concerned, Sun felt that the Chinese had too much of it; indeed, that was what made them 'a heap of loose sand', incapable, as yet, of unifying as a nation. The Chinese did not need more 'liberty', but less; they required a strong hand of authority to educate and discipline them. Sun also saw no place for 'human equality', because the world of nature was characterized by inequality.

The suddenness with which the Qing dynasty disintegrated and the republic arose gave no opportunity to Sun to experiment with the 'three stages': the militarily weak revolutionaries did not win a clear-cut military victory that would have allowed them to introduce a period of political tutelage. Circumstances forced the Revolutionaries to accept Yuan Shikai, the commander-in-chief of the Qing forces, as a compromise president. Yuan, the 'Strong Man of China', unrestrained by any established, viable democratic institution or a popular mandate, became the military dictator of China. After his death in 1916, the country slipped into warlordism for the next decade and Yuan's generals used their troops to usurp local power.

During the politically chaotic warlord era, Marxism–Leninism entered China and, in a manner of speaking, brought to a close the debate on democracy. Sun, betrayed by the West, accepted an alliance with the USSR in 1923 and reorganized his Guomindang (Nationalist Party) along Bolshevik lines and established a party army, with the advice of Moscow. In return for Sun's acceptance of the Chinese Communist Party (CCP) as an ally in his drive to unify China, the Russians agreed that Sun could retain his three principles as the guiding ideology of the party. The success of the Nationalist Revolution in 1928 meant that party dictatorship had finally come to supplant the dynastic system. Significantly, Chiang Kai-Shek, who had assumed the leadership of the Guomindang after Sun's death in 1925, became the *de facto* director of the party and the country, but the second stage of Sun's phased plan of 'tutelage' was not completed till after the Guomindang had been driven to Taiwan by the Communist Revolution in 1949. The Chinese generally accepted the idea that as a practical path to modernization, an authoritarian party could 'tutor' the masses to become democratic, though this was a contradiction in terms.

Sun's three principles, however, were too ill-defined to become the basis of a new popular ideology. In the absence of such a unifying ideology, and because the Nationalists had no programme for social change, the Guomindang's legitimacy was based on its military strength.

Interestingly enough, Chiang Kai-Shek's popularity, as long as it lasted, came from the ready acceptance by the Chinese people of one-man rule.

The twenty years (1928–49) that the Guomindang was in power were not easy years. From its very inauguration, the Nationalist government continuously faced problems of internal unity and external threats of aggression. The re-integration of the country was limited by the endeavours of the erstwhile warlords, who had joined the Guomindang but persisted in retaining their autonomy. It was also hampered by the activities of the CCP. After the Guomindang broke with Russia and the CCP in 1927, the communists went underground, armed themselves and established a parallel government in the hinterland.

The external threat came primarily from the aggressive and expansionist policies of the Japanese. Apart from creating several minor 'incidents', Japan invaded Manchuria in 1931 and established the puppet state of Manchukuo (under the last Manchu emperor who had abdicated in 1912); it annexed Jehol and forced the Guomindang to demilitarize east Hebei province (the area north of Beijing) in 1933. Also, after it had compelled the Guomindang to vacate its forces from the entire province of Hebei in 1935, Japan hinted that it would like the neutralization of five northern provinces. All these actions finally led to the Sino-Japanese war in 1937.

The Japanese very speedily drove the Nationalists out of the rich industrial and agricultural areas of eastern and central China into the interior. Thereafter, there was a general lull in the hostilities, and it was only with the entrance of the US into the war in 1941 that Japan's defeat was ensured.

Before fighting between Japan and China opened, the Guomindang government had made several vigorous efforts to crush the CCP. Had there been no war, the CCP may have been annihilated. The war, however, forced the Guomindang to once again unite with the CCP to fight the invaders. This gave the CCP time to regroup and consolidate its forces. When the inevitable civil war followed the defeat of the Japanese the Guomindang government fell prey to a strong opponent. Faction-ridden, corrupt, and inept, its bureaucracy and troops demoralized by an economy devastated by spiraling inflation, the discredited Nationalist government could not withstand the highly disciplined, tightly organized, popular, and vastly expanded CCP, whose membership and army each numbered over a million.

On 1 October 1949, the People's Republic was established.

The Chinese Communist Party

The Chinese Communist Party was established in 1921. By its very nature the CCP was antagonistic to the ideals of a liberal democracy. That in itself is hardly surprising. What *is* surprising is that the founders of the CCP were intellectuals like Chen Duxiu, who had been the chief proponent of 'Democracy and Science' during the New Culture or May Fourth Movement (1915 to 1922), which he had led. Chen believed that China's weaknesses and ills could be traced to Confucian ideology and that only after the total destruction of Confucianism and its legacy could China achieve a liberal-democratic society. 'If we expect to establish a Western type of modern nation,' wrote Chen, 'then the most basic step is to import the foundation of modern Western society—the faith in the equality of men.' Like Liang, Chen's writings and publications had a profound influence on the Chinese intelligentsia.

In 1919, when the May Fourth Incident took place, Chen joined demonstrations in which the students denounced the warlord government and advocated democracy.

Incidentally, it was same year, 1919, that saw Chen heap praise on the Bolshevik Revolution and suggest that the communist doctrine represented a new historical 'tide'. Chen's writings during the following year showed that he was forsaking liberalism for Marxism–Leninism, and in 1921 Chen became a founder-member of the Chinese Communist Party. How could he, as an intellectual who appeared deeply committed to the ideals of democracy, so casually shift his allegiance to communism? Of course, Chen was not alone in making such a switch; his example is cited only because he was one of the most prominent intellectual figures of his day. A significant number of other nationally recognized intellectuals also began to commit themselves to Marxism. Because of their prestige and authority among the intelligentsia, communism gained quick respect-

4 MAY INCIDENT, 1919: The Chinese Revolution that began at the end of the nineteenth century and is still continuing was motivated to a significant degree by the sense of national humiliation caused by the loss of Chinese territory to foreign powers. The growth of nationalism in the twentieth century made it intolerable for the Chinese intelligentsia to accept the Japanese occupation, during World War I, of German-held Shandong peninsula. But the Chinese, lacking the military means of dislodging the Japanese, could only hope that the Treaty of Versailles would return their territory; after all, China, too, had joined the winning side in the war. The citizenry was stunned when it learned that not only the allied powers but also the warlord government in Beijing had made secret treaties with Japan which would allow the Japanese to retain control over Shandong. On 4 May 1919, 3,000 impassioned students from thirteen Beijing colleges and universities marched to Tiananmen (The Gate of Heavenly Peace— the main southern gate of the Imperial Palace complex; the vast plaza in front of this gate was built later by the communists) and demonstrated against the Treaty. They carried banners, some of them written in blood, attacking the injustice of the Versailles decision, the exploitation of China by the imperialists, and the treacherous Beijing government. The Chinese government arrested 1,000 students but failed to suppress the demonstrations, which then spread to most of the major cities of China. The press took up the cause of the students, whose actions had ignited a mass upsurge of nationalism in urban China; teachers, journalists, lawyers, doctors, shopkeepers, capitalists, and workers joined the protest movement. The government was forced to resign, and China did not sign the Versailles Peace Treaty. This was the first major, 'modern' confrontation between the students and the government of China. The May Fourth Movement, apart from being a symbol of Chinese nationalism and student power, was also associated with a drive for democracy and science. According to Mao Zedong it was the May Fourth Movement that gave birth to the socialist revolution.

ability among many educated Chinese.

Chen, like Liang before him, wanted to see China develop into a strong, independent and prosperous nation; similarly, he was not absolutely committed to any one political creed. Progressive ideas of many political persuasions were being borrowed from the West, so there seemed to be nothing particularly sacrosanct about democracy. For example, in 1920 Chen had toyed with the idea that China could benefit from the adoption of Christianity, because Christianity could be 'progressive' in creating a citizenry with purer feelings of sincerity.

There are several reasons for the sudden popularity of Marxism in China. Till the success of Marxism in Russia, the Chinese, who were seeking a working model in the West which they could imitate, had no reason to consider Marxism as a possible alternative to democracy. China had a minuscule proletariat, and presumably Marxism and the proletariat movement was applicable only to advanced industrialized societies. However, by 1920, when the Bolsheviks had successfully established a socialist government in industrially backward Russia, many Chinese were psychologically ready to accept communism. Not only had the Western democracies disappointed China by their post-war settlement in 1919, but the Chinese intellectuals were also frustrated in their attempts to bring democracy to China. Democracy required a slow evolutionary process that could only build from bottom upwards; but Chinese intellectuals, in a hurry to find a panacea for China's ills, could not wait that long. They were attracted to Marxism, not only because it offered such a panacea but because:

1. It provided a scientific explanation for China's backwardness. China was suffering, not because of its culture, but because it was caught between the exploitative forces of warlord feudalism and foreign imperialism. By accepting Marxism, it was no longer necessary to repudiate the national heritage of Confucianism and create

a destructive sense of cultural rootlessness. China did not have to reject its past, but put it in the context of universal historical change.

2. Marxism–Leninism fitted the subconscious habits of mind created by Confucianism: (a) A single theory justified all socio-political action; (b) policies emanated from the top and guided the action of all peoples at the bottom; (c) the revolution would be led by an elitist group of intellectuals whose claim to power, like that of the scholar-gentry, would rest on their knowledge of the true doctrine. This leadership group did not have to worry about understanding the peasantry, or the intricacies of commerce and trade; they needed only to comprehend the doctrine.

3. Lenin's theory of imperialism gave a historic role to colonial and semi-colonial countries, such as China. By carrying out anti-imperialist revolutions, these countries would hasten the downfall of capitalism in advanced industrial countries and, thus, further the cause of world revolution. With the collapse of imperialism, the colonial and semi-colonial countries could move onto the socialist stage, bypassing the capitalist stage.

4. Marxism–Leninism provided the Chinese intellectuals a blueprint for action.

Between 1921 and 1949, though the CCP's internal organization remained similar to that of the Bolshevized Guomindang, its ideology underwent many changes. Most, if not all, were associated with Mao Zedong. Breaking with orthodox Marxism–Leninism, the CCP evolved a new revolutionary approach that accepted the *peasants* as the backbone of the revolution. Instead of being proletariat-based and working outward from the cities, the CCP strategy was to strengthen 'revolutionary bases' in the countryside, to surround and then capture the cities, the strongholds of the Guomindang.

In this and other tactics considered unique to him, Mao was both Confucian and communist. The Confucian theory of rebellion justified the overthrow of an emperor who had allowed the political arrangement to deteriorate and the peasant to be exploited beyond endurable limits. The heavenly mandate to rule could be withdrawn because 'Heaven hears as the people hear, Heaven sees as the people see'. Such traditional rebellions, although they may have been led by a popular religious sect, aimed at restoring an ideal, secular Confucian ethical and moral government. Mao, too, identified politics and government with ethics, and he did lead a massive peasant rebellion for a re-dedication of the government to the welfare of the people.

Every Confucian worthy of his name had exhorted the rulers and the ruling elites to 'serve the people'. 'The enlightened ruler,' said Mencius, the great Confucian philosopher of the fourth century BC, 'regulates the livelihood of the people so as to make sure that they have sufficient (means) with which to serve their parents, and also to support their wives and children; that in good years they should be abundantly satisfied, and in bad years they should be protected from the danger of perishing.' To guarantee this, Mencius advocated an agricultural system in which all peasants would be allotted an equal amount of land. The influence of this socialistic idea was profound, and repeated attempts were made by various dynasties to establish an 'equal-field' system. Though private ownership of land became the norm after the tenth century AD, the earlier ideal never died. The Taiping rebels, who occupied a large territory in central China around 1850 and established their own dynasty (1851–64), were the last to experiment with the Mencian land system in the declining years of imperial China. However, Sun Yat-Sen also had borrowed Mencius' term, 'the people's livelihood' (translated as 'socialism'), as one of his three principles.

People, to the Confucians, meant the peasantry and so it did to Mao. Furthermore, the roots of tradition are visible in Mao's message: 'Serve the people wholeheartedly and never for a moment divorce ourselves from the masses, to proceed in all cases from the interest of the people and not from one's self-interest or from the interests of a small group.' The pronounced goal of Mao's revolution was not the emancipation of the proletariat but a redistribution of the land holdings so that all the tillers of the soil could gain an equitable source of livelihood. In this respect, Marxism–Leninism, which Mao hardly understood with any clarity, when he began his revolutionary career, did not destroy Mao's traditional view of a 'benevolent government'. Mao accepted the Confucian assumption that the people were good at heart and only acquired evil ways if not properly instructed.

Mao was also aware, consciously or unconsciously, of the fact that in a successful rebellion the masses of China transferred their loyalty and obedience from the evil emperor to a single charismatic leader who led the rebellion. This leader became the founding emperor of a new dynasty, and then as 'Son of Heaven' rightfully claimed their loyalty and obedience. So it is not surprising that even before the People's Republic was established, Mao encouraged the cult of personality and emerged as 'The Leader' and 'The Teacher' of his people. As a document of the party claimed in 1945:

> Ever since its birth in 1921, the Communist Party of China has made the integration of the universal truth of Marxism–Leninism with the concrete practice of the Chinese revolution the guiding principle in all its work, and Comrade Mao Zedong's theory and practice of the Chinese revolution represent this integration . . . . In the course of its struggle the party has produced its own leader, Comrade Mao Zedong (who has) creatively applied the scientific theory of Marxism–Leninism, the acme of human wisdom to China . . .

This myth of Mao's emperor-like infallibility became the basic fact of the country's political life till Mao's death. Many years later, during the period of the Great Proletarian Cultural Revolution (1966–69) Mao used the cult of personality to incite the public to attack the party leaders who had opposed his policies. In the process, the party structure was damaged and party prestige destroyed. When a foreign journalist, an old friend of Mao's, asked Mao to comment on the criticism that he was building up a cult of personality, Mao said: 'It was hard for the people to overcome the habits of 3,000 years of emperor-worshipping tradition.' The question, of course, is: did Mao try to destroy that habit? The answer is both 'Yes' and 'No'. Mao did want the people to discard traditional vices, including their penchant to blindly follow authority; and he did emphasize the Marxist notion of class 'struggle' over the Confucian ideal of 'harmony'. Yet, he promoted the people's passive, unquestioning acceptance of *his* authority so that they could unthinkingly reject the authority of his 'enemies' and *struggle* against them.

What were Mao's views on democracy? Mao was a populist and had a solid faith in the capacity of the 'people' to carry out the revolution. He also believed that it was necessary for the leaders to maintain close contact with the masses. So Mao worked out the doctrine of the 'mass-line' as a reinforcement to the organizational principle of 'democratic centralism'. The doctrine is ambiguous. Though it states the party's dependence on the masses and the need for the party to be in constant contact with the masses, it reaffirms the need for central control. The party cadres, according to the mass-line theory, find out what the masses want or do not want, turn their inchoate ideas into policies, then 'go to the masses and propagate and explain these ideas *until the masses embrace them as their own*'. To Mao this amounted to the people's participation in the government. In actual practice, the cadres found it difficult to locate the 'scattered and unsystematic ideas' of the masses, but far easier to propagate the policies decided at the centre. Unlike the vague mass-line, Mao's concept of democratic centralism was much clearer; 'The Communist Party not only needs democracy, but needs centralization even more. (Comrades seem to) forget the system of democratic centralism, in which the minority is subordinate to the majority, *the lower level to the higher level, the part to the whole, and the entire membership to the Central Committee.*'

In June 1945, on the eve of the establishment of the People's Republic, Mao elaborated his thesis on the 'people's democratic dictatorship'. He postulated that in the communist government the party would lead a united front formed of the workers, peasants, the petty bourgeoisie, and the national (patriotic) bourgeoisie—'the people'. The people would enforce 'their dictatorship over the running dogs of imperialism—the landlord class and bureaucratic bourgeoisie, as well as the representatives of those classes, the Kuomintang (Guomindang) reactionaries and their accomplices . . . . The state apparatus, including the army, the police and the courts is the instrument by which one class oppresses another . . . . We definitely do not apply a policy of benevolence to the reactionaries . . . . .' Since anyone found wanting in socialist virtue could be condemned as a member of the reactionary class (as was frequently done later), a 'people' person could be transformed into a 'non-people' person with the greatest facility. Without any legal safeguards, the individual under these conditions could exercise no independent judgement, but proved his/her political reliability by conforming to the current political line. The system did not allow for even a loyal critic.

After the revolution had succeeded, with the establishment of the People's Republic of China (PRC), Mao's communist party revealed its greatest weakness: the party had no roots in any segment of the population—*it represented nobody but itself.* The historical environment in which the party had developed and grown had made it heavily dependent on the peasantry. But Mao, whatever his psychological predisposition, was against 'peasant consciousness'; regardless of how he had manipulated Marxism, he was a true believer in socialism. Having gained national power, the party had to instruct the people in the new socialist ideology of Maoism. In his article on People's Democratic Dictatorship, Mao makes particular reference to the 'education' of the peasantry and the consolidation of socialism through the 'socialization of agriculture'. The party supposedly represented urban labour, the proletariat. But since it had been out of touch with the cities since 1930, it had no roots in that class. As a result, the party declared in 1949 that the working class must also be re-educated.

> Marxism holds that the working class is most reliable. Generally speaking, this is correct, but we still have some specific problems. So we must strive *to enable our working class to become completely reliable* (emphasis added). If we ignore these problems and rely on the workers without doing any work among them, they won't necessarily be reliable.

Of course, the bourgeoisie and the intellectuals needed to be re-educated. Under the People's Democratic Dictatorship, declared Mao, the people can 'educate and re-mould themselves on a countrywide scale by democratic methods and, *with everyone taking part,* shake off the influence of domestic and foreign reactionaries (which is still very strong . . .), rid themselves of the bad habits and ideas acquired in the old society, not allow themselves to be led astray by reactionaries, and continue to advance—to advance toward a socialist and communist society'.

Evidently all classes and all peoples needed to be re-educated, and only the party could give them the right direction and guidance. However, when trouble rose later, Mao discovered that the party itself needed re-education. Who was to teach the teachers? At that stage it became abundantly clear that only Mao, 'the Great Helmsman', possessed knowledge of the 'True Doctrine'. Democracy, socialist or capitalist, could hardly develop under such conditions.

Post-imperial China has yet to discard the traditional Chinese view that government is of men more than laws, and that all power emanates from above, from a single, emperor-like, supreme ruler, who is superior to all other people. Such were the qualities ascribed to Sun Yat-Sen, Chiang Kai-Shek, and Mao Zedong. These leaders were not legitimized by any legal structures but by their ideological message and morality.

Therefore, it comes as no surprise that, after the Tiananmen Square massacre, even Deng Xiaoping, the current supreme leader of China, who had once criticized the deification of Mao, has sought to restore order by encouraging the party to portray him (Deng) as 'China's greatest hero'.

2

Mao Zedong and the Soviet Model The People's Republic: 1949–57

The establishment of the People's Republic of China (1 October 1949) fulfilled one of the main goals of the Chinese revolution: it marked the end of the hundred years of national humiliation and unequal relations with the big powers. The new government was sufficiently strong militarily to re-exert China's sovereignty and to insist that all nations wanting to establish friendly relations with the PRC must do so on the basis of strict equality, mutual benefit and mutual respect. Imperialist interests secured by Britain in Tibet and inherited by independent India did create a temporary problem, but this was resolved when the Chinese moved their armies into Tibet in 1951 after having made a settlement with New Delhi. The Soviet Union, the PRC's closest and most important ally, retained even after 1949 some of the privileges acquired through 'unequal' treaties; but these also were surrendered within a decade. This left British Hong Kong and Taiwan (where the Nationalists had fled) as the sole remaining territories not yet united with the motherland. The communists also regained China's fiscal independence by renouncing all foreign loans contracted by the previous governments.

The Chinese people regained a sense of pride in 1949. What heightened their self-esteem even more, and brought them the respect of the outside world, was Beijing's involvement in the Korean War. The young republic had had hardly any time to settle down when the war began in 1950, and many feared that China was ill-prepared to face the massive military might of the United States. Although the war did prove very costly (nearly a million Chinese soldiers died), the Chinese, to everyone's surprise, fought the United States to a standstill. The war, incidentally, also helped the communists to get rid of their enemies within the country (pro-US and pro-Guomindang elements) and thus eased their path to socialism.

The International Context of China's Development An Overview

On the negative side, Sino-American hostilities resulted in the US recognition of Chiang Kai-Shek's regime in Taiwan as the 'true' government of all China. For the next twenty years the US prohibited virtually all trade and financial dealings with the People's Republic, as well as any cultural and academic exchanges. America also pressured its allies to place an embargo on the export to China of certain strategic goods.

This forced China to rely heavily on the Soviet Union and the socialist bloc for the much-needed industrial and financial aid. However, Mao Zedong, for political and ideological reasons, ended this dependence on the Soviet Union in the early 1960s. Mao's desire to see China follow his personal vision of development and modernization, epitomized by his economic-cum-social experiment of the Great Leap Forward (GLF) in 1958, led to a diplomatic break with the Soviet Union in the mid-1960s. A few years later, in 1966, when Mao launched his second major experiment with social change and economic autarky, the Great Proletarian Cultural Revolution (GPCR), China isolated itself from the world community for several years.

A major shift in foreign policy took place in the 1970s, symbolized by President Richard Nixon's dramatic visit to China in 1972, which heralded the beginning of a process of Sino-American rapprochement. Most of America's allies hastily followed the US lead, withdrawing recognition from Taipei and opening diplomatic relations with Beijing. China had re-entered the family of nations and shifted to a more 'normal' programme of modernization, which entailed the import of technology, expertise, and capital from the advanced capitalist countries. This programme, hesitantly started in the last years of Mao's rule, gained tremendous momentum under the aegis of Deng Xiaoping.

Internal Developments

The real problems that Mao Zedong and his party faced in 1949 were not external but internal. The communists were confronted with a fragmented country, that lacked both social and political integration. China's economy, disrupted and damaged by war and civil war, was in shambles. To take one example, the wholesale price index had risen from 100 in 1937 to 2,617,781 in 1947! The economic infrastructure, at the very basic level, lay shattered: dams, canals, roads, railroads, and factories needed urgent repairs and renovations. The country's population had exploded to the staggering figure of 500,000,000 and hundreds of millions of the poorer peasants were living in abject misery, subject to extremes of hunger, disease, and social exploitation.

By any calculation, the tasks were formidable. To the credit of the new government, it managed to solve most of the country's primary problems with amazing speed. Today China's economy is doing far better than that of India, a comparably large Asian state; not only is the general standard of living of over 1,000,000,000 Chinese people higher than that of the 820,000,000 people of India, but, in sharp contrast to India, the life of the poorest Chinese peasant communities, at the very bottom of society, is no longer insecure.

Why then the 'Spring Massacre'? The answer to that question can be traced to the manner in which Mao personalized power and correlated his idiosyncratic ideology with modernization. This kept the country from developing some of the key institutions (such as a legal order that would have guaranteed individual rights) that are needed for conflict resolution. If they had been established, they would have contributed to the stability of the state. Unfortunately, even after Mao's death, and the demythification of Maoism by Deng Xiaoping, the Maoist style of leadership has not been eliminated.

China and the Soviet Model

From 1947 to 1956, when the CCP was dismantling the old order and replacing it with their new system, the Maoist model and the Soviet model were used concurrently. The situation did not produce major conflicts because Mao's ideas and practices were being applied, primarily, to the countryside, while the Soviet model was being copied in the cities. The Maoist technique of indoctrination through 'mass campaigns' overlapped the two areas, but even that did not cause any substantial dissension. It was only in 1956, when the 'transition to socialism' had been successfully completed, that Mao began to exert the superiority of his ideology and question the utility of the Soviet model for China's future development. It was then that other leaders of the CCP started to disagree with Mao.

During the period 1949 to 1956, regardless of the ubiquitous presence of Soviet advisors in China and the importance of Soviet aid, Mao Zedong's position remained unchallenged. Part of the reason for this was Mao's early admission of the party's inexperience in handling sophisticated nationwide economic and administrative problems and his readiness to accept advice and guidance from the Soviet Union. The CCP faced three main tasks: (1) the consolidation of party control over the countryside and the socialization of agriculture; (2) the reorientation of urban institutions to conform to socialistic goals and the training of personnel to handle urban-based economic, administrative and social affairs; and (3) the re-education of the people so that they could comprehend the new ideology and embrace socialist values and practices. Mao and the other leaders hoped that the third task would be accomplished in the process of fulfilling the first two.

The first goal was achieved with the land reform programme, which the CCP was well equipped to handle because of its past experience. The job was not easy, because the unexpectedly quick victory in 1949 had suddenly brought vast areas of Guomindang-governed territory under CCP control—areas that had never known the communists, or even heard of Mao Zedong. The peasants in these areas were still in awe of the landlords and suspicious of the new government. But the CCP quickly infiltrated each village with units of the People's Liberation Army (PLA) and members of the CCP. While the CCP cadres organized peasant associations and propagated the new ideology, the PLA helped to enforce law and order and acted as an instrument of coercion where necessary.

The peasant associations held mass meetings in which the achievements of the CCP and Mao Zedong were extolled and the new order explained. In the beginning the cadres usually found it difficult to get the poorer peasants to speak up against the landlords. The CCP strategy was to select a number of the very poorest of the peasants, win them over by assuring them that the landlords had little leverage against the power of the CCP and give them prominent positions in the association. These outspoken activists would encourage the other traditionally intimidated sections of the village community to join them. Finally, a rally would be organized where all the peasants were incited to publicly attack the landlords (targeted as 'class enemies', 'feudal reactionaries' and 'despots') for their past 'evil', exploitative activities. The meetings ended with the landlords being deprived of their lands and receiving various degrees of punishment, ranging from imprisonment to execution—many were beaten to death on the spot by the aroused masses. Responsible estimates of the number of landlords killed range from 2,000,000 to 5,000,000.

The land taken away from the landlords was then redistributed among the peasantry according to the class in which they had been ranked by the communist work teams; the four class designations were: rich peasant, middle peasant, poor peasant, and landless labourer. The intention of this Maoist technique of induced antagonism was to politicize the masses in order to make them discard their old habits of subservience to the local elites and to get them to wholeheartedly support the CCP. In other words, the masses were encouraged to become active and loyal participants in the new system.

That the communists had succeeded in their endeavours became abundantly clear in the next few years when the government guided the peasants through various stages of collectivization: from 'mutual aid teams' (four to five families helping each other on their fields), through semi-socialist Agricultural Producers' Cooperatives (APCs; twenty to thirty families pooling their land, tools, and labour resources), to fully socialist APCs (the pooling of assets of 200 to 300 households, the assets owned by the cooperative). Though the last stage was completed only in 1957, the conclusion of the second stage in 1956 was considered as the 'transition to socialism' in the countryside.

For the second task of socializing the cities, the CCP depended heavily on the Soviet model, and in a very short time China had copied the Soviet military and governmental system, the educational system, the economic and industrial organizations, and the legal system. The Soviets firmly believed that economic development should be *planned* and that it should be both centrally directed and centrally controlled. As a result, Soviet-style economic ministries, a State Planning Commission, and other structures which ensured the state's control over economic resources, were established before the First Five-Year-Plan (FYP) was inaugurated in 1953. By 1957 when the Plan ended, a secure base had been laid for China's future industrial development.

In the meantime, the CCP had forced all the citizens in the urban areas to become members of one or more communist-controlled organizations set up in their work places and residential neighbourhoods and had enrolled all the workers in communist-run unions. In the process of bringing socialism to the cities, the CCP used Mao's formula of 'the people's democratic dictatorship' to separate the large number of good 'people' from their 'class enemies', the 'non-people' (the 'bourgeois reactionaries' and 'counter-revolutionaries'). Then, through various discrete campaigns directed at pro-Guomindang elements, capitalists, industrialists, bourgeoisie, and corrupt bureaucrats, the 'people' were persuaded to uncover hidden 'non-people' and denounce them in mass trials, which, as in the case of the landlords, led to 'confessions' by the 'criminals' and their punishment. Nearly 1,000,000 were executed. Nobody in the cities any longer had any doubts about where, or in whose hands, power and authority lay. By 1956, all private business enterprises had been nationalized, and though many of the capitalists were retained as managers and directors of the companies they once owned, the 'capitalist class' had disappeared. The transition to socialism in the urban arena had been successfully completed.

One of the troublesome problems the CCP came to face in the cities was that of the intellectuals and education. In spite of Mao Zedong's instinctive distrust of specialists and specialization, after the establishment of the PRC the party needed a large body of trained elite to man the bureaucracy, organize the service and commercial sectors, manage the industries, and guide general and adult education. Since the party could not start from scratch, it had to accept the intelligentsia that had been left

Excerpt from the opera

'THE WHITE–HAIRED GIRL'*

(The opera deals with the story of a wicked landlord named Huang 'who oppressed the peasants cruelly. One of his old tenants had a daughter aged seventeen, Xi-er, who took his fancy; so on the pretext of collecting rent he contrived to drive her father to commit suicide, then carried off the girl, and when he had her in his clutches raped her. Later she became pregnant. When this happened, he decided to murder her'. The girl escaped and found a mountain cave to hide in. There she lived with her child. 'Nursing her hatred and bitterness, she remained several years in the cave. Because she went cold and hungry, was seldom in the sun, and had no salt in her diet, her hair turned white.' She stole food from the offerings made in the local temple. Villagers who sometimes got a glimpse of her thought that she was a white-haired spirit. It was only after the CCP had liberated the area and rehabilitated her, that the tragedy of Xi-er's life become public and Huang was tried for his crimes.

The opera written before 1949, became very popular and was used extensively in the land reform programme.)

Scene III (Peasant Mass Meeting)

Gongs sound offstage. Shouts are heard: 'Come to the meeting!' 'The meeting's at the gate of the Huang family ancestral hall.'

(Singing offstage):

Age-old injustice must be avenged,
And a thousand years' wrongs be set right!
Xi-er was forced to become a ghost,
Becomes human again today!
Crushing rents must be reduced,

* See, Ho Ching-Chih and Ting Yi, *The White-Haired Girl*, Peking: Foreign Languages Press, 1954. (The original text has been amended for quotation.)

The grain extorted must be restored!
Those who suffered their whole life long,
Will stand up and become masters today!

How much of our blood have you sucked?
How much have you drunk of our sweat?
How much of our grain did you steal?
How much of our gold did you get?
How long have you tricked and opposed us?
How many deaths at your door?
Today we shall settle scores with you,
Settle every score!

(The curtain parts and Huang is seen standing on the platform with his head bowed. Angry villagers are grouped in front of him. The accusations made by the villagers are sung in operatic form . . .)

FIRST PEASANT: You pretend to reduce the rent, but it's all a lie!

SECOND PEASANT: You take the land back on the sly!

THIRD PEASANT: When you've rumours to spread, you rattle away!

FOURTH PEASANT: When you hound folk to death, you've nothing to say!

(Huang mumbles and wants to justify himself)

FIFTH PEASANT: Landlord Huang do you argue still?
To pretend to be crazy will serve you ill!

SIXTH PEASANT: Landlord Huang, I tell you.
The bad old times have got to stop!
We common folk are on the top!

ALL *(in chorus)*: Today the world is ours instead!
Murderers must atone for the dead!
Pay what you owe to the folks you've bled!
We'll have your blood for the blood you've shed!

(Seeing the landlord thus humbled, the peasant women are encouraged to step forth with their bitter accusations: Huang had broken the legs of one woman's father, the brother of another had fallen to his death building the landlord's tower, one's son had drowned repairing a dike, and so on.)

THE CROWD: We want vengeance for Xi-er

XI-ER: I want vengeance for all that happened
My wrongs are too many to tell!
They're a mountain that can't be levelled!
A sea that can't be drained!
But what's caused such a great change
That I can beard my enemy today?
Landlord Huang–
To be cut to pieces is too good for you!

ALL: To be cut to pieces is too good for you!
To be cut to pieces is too good for you!
To be cut to pieces is too good for you!

(Xi-er then recites the history of her life: how she was raped, how Huang tried to sell her off as a prostitute, how she escaped to the mountain cave, how she lived in isolation, etc., etc. At the end of the story, the villagers' passions have risen to such a degree that they rush forward to beat Huang to death. The district head stops them, saying that public trial will be held later. One can imagine how that trial will end.)

over from the Nationalist republic. This elite and the educational system which had fostered it, however, were both considered to be tainted by 'bourgeois thinking'. To ensure that the intelligentsia changed its 'bourgeois' habits of thought, the party carried out horrendous 'thought reform' programmes which used techniques of 'brainwashing' (a literal translation of the popular Chinese term) to cleanse the mind of all non-communist ideologies.

The process of brainwashing involved several stages. First, the subject was 'struggled against' by his peers, who criticized him for past errors and actions that reflected incorrect thinking; then the subject was given time to 'study' the new ideology and ruminate over his past misdoings, make 'self-criticism', and 'confess' his 'crimes'. If the confession was considered to be insincere (i.e., if it indicated that the person still had not totally lost his self-esteem and sense of individualism), the subject was isolated from family and friends, given more Maoist literature to study, and forced to write more confessions. This period of privation, insecurity, and inner tension led to a chastening of the spirit and a genuine desire to 'belong' to the new communist brotherhood. If this process was not successful in bringing the desired change in the state of the subject's mind, he would be sent to work for a few months in a factory or in the fields to labour with the masses and undergo 'thought reform through labour'. (The theory was that intellectuals were divorced from 'practice' and needed to labour with their hands before they could appreciate the importance of labour and the labouring classes, whom they were meant to serve.) If that too failed, or if it was recognized from the very beginning that the subject was sufficiently important and that his execution would set 'a negative example' for his peers, a mass trial would be held and the subject publicly shot.

Through these policies the CCP brought the intellectuals into line and hoped that their thoughts had been remoulded and their hearts won over. Most of the intellectuals who suffered thought reform had been educated in the Nationalist era. They had shifted their allegiance from the corrupt Guomindang regime to the CCP, because they had been eager for the emergence of a powerful, reunited China. Many of them had willingly given up Western-style ideals of democracy and offered full-hearted support to the communist party. But for all their left-leaning views (some had even joined the party), it would soon become clear that they were not ready to sacrifice their intellectual freedom. However, the CCP's ruthless policies forced them to offer lip service to the party and display an outward conformity to the party line.

By 1956 the party felt that since the transition to socialism had been made and the enemy 'classes' eliminated (including the 'counterrevolutionary' intellectuals), the time had come to relax controls over the intellectuals. An alienated intelligentsia could not be expected to make the positive contribution that a rapidly developing country needed. Indeed, there was a growing recognition within the party that it had been too heavy-handed in its dealings with the intelligentsia and that it should change its policies. This was spelled out by premier Zhou Enlai in his 'Report on the Question of Intellectuals' (January 1956). After declaring that, 'only a very small number of (intellectuals) were counter-revolutionaries', Zhou went on to say that:

> Facts clearly pointed out to the intellectuals that except for standing together with the working class and the Chinese Communist Party, there was no other way out for them. It is therefore necessary, as it is also possible, to unite with the intellectuals . . . *We must confess that there are many shortcomings in our work* . . . (we have failed to place) confidence in intellectuals who deserve it, such as forbidding them to visit factories which they should see and barring them from information they should possess.

Mao probably had no quarrel with this assessment, but in this action of the party to coopt the intellectuals to help run the centralized state machine, Mao discerned the ascendancy of the Soviet model. Mao's ideas and practices had begun to lose ground because they were no longer applicable in a paradigm that presumed the completion of the revolutionary stage of social upheaval and expected that for a long time to come the nation needed a systematic, well-planned approach to economic modernization. Acceptance of this model meant that further socialist transformation of society would have to be delayed till economic modernization had taken place.

It was anathema to Mao that the party, instead of depending on the 'creative enthusiasm' of the masses and the 'mass-line', was developing Soviet-style command leadership which gave unchallenged power to the party and presumed that all decisions were to be taken at the top and passed down through hierarchically-structured organs of state. Such a system gave prime importance to elitist technocrats, placed authority in the hands of bureaucrats and managers, and depended on salary differentials and monetary incentives.

Mao was not against economic development, but he saw China becoming a victim of an 'economic first' approach that would spell the end of his revolution. Mao believed in permanent, or continuous, revolution. A society, according to Mao, was never free of internal contradictions, and it was through 'ceaseless change and upheaval' that these contradictions could be advantageously resolved. Only by following this process could society progressively achieve a higher and higher level of political consciousness and, thus, ensure the evolution of the true 'socialist man'. In practice this meant that mass mobilization campaigns could not be eliminated. Therefore, instead of increased centralization, Mao wanted to see a greater decentralization of authority in the arena of production; instead of a command approach, Mao wanted the party to encourage mass participation in management and decision making. Mao was also against monetary incentives because they produced a capitalist mentality; Mao wanted them replaced with 'ideological' incentives.

Mao realized that unless he moved quickly and re-exerted his ideology he would lose control of the party and the revolutionary momentum. Since other CCP leaders were increasingly identifying themselves with the Soviet economic development strategy, somehow he had to prove that his policies were better than those of the Soviet-style planners.

Mao made his first move in the countryside, where the relentless demands of the heavy-industry-oriented First FYP were having a negative impact. The Plan had allocated a very small fraction of the development budget to the rural sector, with the result that Chinese agricultural growth was falling far behind that of industry. Yet, industrialization depended upon agriculture, so the question before the party was how to increase agricultural production without making any large shift of investment funds from industry to agriculture. Mao's solution was to speed up collectivization in the countryside. Other party leaders did not agree, because they believed that only a gradual, step-by-step approach would ensure that the country was ready for further collectivization. The establishment of advanced cooperatives would necessarily result in the emergence of large farming units which, to be fully productive, required tractors and other machinery, chemical fertilizers, and electricity, as well as the services of technicians. But this presumed that the industrial capacity of the country, and its educational facilities, had advanced to such a degree that the urban sector could serve the countryside. Indeed, by mid-1955 only fifteen per cent of the rural population had joined semi-socialist APC's and the goal of the First FYP was to place only one-third of the peasant households in these elementary cooperatives by 1957.

Mao rejected this slow-paced approach. He firmly believed that ideologically-inspired masses did not need machines to achieve production goals. He also feared that halting the rural revolution at this stage would only result in the re-emergence of capitalism. Had not the scarcities in the countryside, coupled with the authoritarianism of the cadres (who were zealously collecting agricultural taxes to fulfil their quotas), compelled many poor peasants to sell their lands to a growing class of wealthier land owners? Mao found this state of affairs intolerable. So, instead of trying to further convince the party leaders to change their policy, Mao spoke directly to provincial party secretaries and propaganda officials in July 1955:

> What exists in the countryside today is capitalist ownership by the rich peasants and a vast sea of private ownership by the individual peasants. As is clear to everyone, the spontaneous forces of capitalism have been growing steadily in the countryside in recent years, with new rich peasants springing up everywhere and many well-to-do middle peasants striving to become rich peasants. On the other hand, many poor peasants are still living in poverty for lack of sufficient means of production, with some in debt and others selling or renting out their land . . . . There is no solution to this problem except on a new basis . . . the socialist transformation *of the whole of agriculture*.

Mao censured the party leaders who opposed him, bursting out that: 'some of our comrades are tottering along like a woman with bound feet and constantly complaining, "You are going too fast".' Many years later it came to light that Mao was referring to Liu Shaoqi (the senior-most party leader after Mao) and other high-ranking party figures.

These party leaders could not stop Mao from leading the lower-level cadres to mobilize the peasantry and start a massive collectivization campaign. The results of this action were astounding. By the end of 1956 virtually all the rural families had joined semi-socialist APCs, while some of them had gone even further and formed fully socialist APCs. Indeed, by early 1957, ninety per cent of the peasantry was in advanced level APCs. Mao had re-exerted his policies and shown that planners and technocrats could be replaced with the 'boundless enthusiasm' of the masses. But in doing so Mao had discarded the vital principle of 'democratic centralism', putting himself above the party and undermining party unity.

Although Mao's ambitious plan was not as great a success as he had hoped (many peasants slaughtered their draught animals and livestock and showed little ardour in working on collectivized fields), his policy had prevailed. One wonders what Li Fuchun, the chairman of the State Planning Commission, and other pro-planning leaders felt about this development; in his report in mid-1955 Li had calculated that it would take fifteen years to 'fulfil this fundamental task of transition to socialism' in the countryside.

However, Mao's victory was confined to the countryside; if the Maoist model was to prevail over the whole country, somehow Mao had to rupture the close relations between the CCP and Moscow. As long as China accepted the leadership role of the Soviet Union, Mao could not be truly 'independent' to exercise his will over the national development strategy. Fortunately for Mao, Khrushchev's denunciation of Stalin in the Soviet twentieth Party Congress in 1956 provided just the opportunity he had been seeking to begin an attack on the Soviet model.

Khrushchev's condemnation of Stalin for putting himself above the Soviet communist party and developing a 'cult of personality' made it difficult for the Chinese leaders to explain to their followers the CCP's earlier glorification of Stalin. It also reflected adversely on Mao's leadership style because he had been assiduously building up his own cult of personality. Furthermore, Khrushchev, without consulting Mao, had enunciated his views on 'peaceful coexistence' with the capitalist nations and *detente* with the USA.

This put Mao in a quandary. He would either have to accept Moscow's new foreign policy line, in the manner of Moscow's East European client states, and give up his pet notions of a continuing confrontation between the socialist and capitalist blocs, or reject Moscow's stand and break away from the bloc. Mao decided to follow the latter course.

Mao's first expression of revolt against Moscow's ideological authority came in an article in the *People's Daily* (April 1956): 'On the Historical Experience of the Dictatorship of the Proletariat'. The article praised Stalin as a 'great Marxist-Leninist revolutionary' who had made many important contributions to the development of socialism, and whose merits were greater than his faults. The article accepted the criticism that Stalin had made 'some serious mistakes' in his later life, but put them down to his having divorced himself from the masses. This was something which Mao, presumably, would never do.

As for Stalin's misuse of 'class-warfare' to purge his opponents, the article pointed out that 'society at all times develops through continual contradictions', and to 'deny contradictions, is to deny dialectics .... Viewed in this light, the existence of contradictions between the individual and the collective in a socialist society is nothing strange'. The Russians found this thesis, which suggested that social injustice and conflicts of interest between the leaders and the led could continue even under socialism, unacceptable. When the Chinese article was reproduced in *Pravda*, the 'contradiction' section was deleted.

Mao's article accepted Khrushchev's attack on the 'cult of the individual', but added that such a development took place only when the 'mass-line' was ignored. By implication, Mao's cult of personality fell in a different category! The article also asserted that,

> Marxist–Leninists hold that party leaders play a big role in history. *The peoples and their parties need forerunners who are able to*

> *represent the interests and will of the people, stand in front of their historic struggles and serve as their leaders.*

That Mao had made up his mind to modify, if not abandon, Soviet-style development became further apparent in a secret speech, 'On the Ten Great Relationships', given in April 1956, but not published for twenty years.

Mao divided China's problems of modernization and change into ten major contradictions, which included contradictions between industry and agriculture, heavy and light industry, coastal and inland industries, economic and defence constructions, and the centre and the regions. To properly handle these contradictions, Mao suggested that instead of strengthening existing, strong, industrial centres in the coastal region, China should establish ninety per cent of future heavy industry inland. Economically this would not be as efficient as the Soviet Model, but it would industrialize the whole country and help to turn the peasants into workers. In this Maoist model the size of the party and government organizations were to be cut back by two-thirds (to avoid Soviet-style bureaucratization of these institutions), controls and authority were to be decentralized, and production initiative was to come from below, from workers and peasants rather than from the managerial class above.

The tenth 'great' relationship, 'the relationship between China and other countries', is particularly relevant to an understanding of Mao's anti-Soviet stand. 'We propose learning the good things of other countries', said Mao, 'not the bad. In the past some of us were unclear about this and also learned the bad things . . . . We must do as Mencius says: "When speaking to the mighty, look on them with contempt." (an obvious reference to the USSR) We must develop the spirit which we had during the "Resist America, Aid Korea" campaign, of looking with contempt on the imperialists.'*

On a different occasion, in a speech in 1958, Mao provided a much clearer insight into his view of the Soviet model:

---

* This and the next three quotes are from Stuart Schram, Ed., *Chairman Mao Speaks to the People*, New York: Pantheon, 1974.

> In the period following the liberation of the whole country, dogmatism (i.e., the Soviet style of doing things) made its appearance both in economic and in cultural and educational work . . . In economic work dogmatism primarily manifested itself in heavy industry and planning. Since we did not understand these things and had absolutely no experience, all we could do in our ignorance was to import foreign methods . . . We did not even study our own experience of education in the Liberated Areas. The same applied to our public health work, with the result that I couldn't have eggs or chicken soup for three years because an article appeared in the Soviet Union which said that one shouldn't eat them.

Thus, in 1956, having already succeeded in forcing the party to alter its policies towards the rural sector, Mao turned his attention to what he considered to be 'shortcomings' in the urban-based Soviet-style development strategy. The party leaders agreed with him that some changes in the investment pattern were called for, but they resisted accepting Mao's model and abdicating their faith in bureaucratically-controlled centralized planning. Indeed, while Mao, in mid-1956, was trying his best to convince the party to apply his development tactics, the technocrats were busy drawing up the Second FYP. At the eighth Party Congress, held in September 1956, Liu Shaoqi and his colleagues not only ignored Mao's unorthodox economic plan advocated in the Ten Great Relationships, but even tried to dilute Mao's authority by deleting the clause from the Party Constitution that said the party was guided by the 'Thought of Mao Zedong'. Liu, in his report to the Congress, also made an oblique attack on Mao's penchant for ignoring the party centre:

> Every leader must be good at listening patiently to, and taking into deliberate consideration, opinions contrary to his own, in order to resolutely approve opposing views if reasonable, or whatever is reasonable in them . . . . Only in this way can we *achieve collective leadership and party unity in deed, and not in name only, and assure greater flourishing of its organization and cause.*

It is at this stage that Mao appears to have decided to take more direct action against the party, but he had to wait a year before circumstances were ripe for him to do so. One of Mao's biggest problems was that he had all along linked 'contradictions' with 'class struggle'; but now that the transition to socialism had been made and, theoretically, the exploiting classes had been eliminated, he had no plank left to carry on his style of induced class conflict. Two developments, which Mao fostered, were to help him make a comeback in 1957: the party rectification campaign, and the Hundred Flowers movement.

Party leaders generally agreed with Mao that the rapid expansion of the party bureaucracy had led to the evils of 'subjectivism', 'bureaucratism', and 'sectarianism'. Broadly speaking, 'subjectivism' was manifested in a dogmatic application of Soviet theory and practice without any consideration of the fact that Chinese 'reality' and needs called for a more flexible approach; 'bureaucratism' was evidenced in the elitist attitude of the officials who divorced themselves from the masses; and 'sectarianism' led party members to behave as if they were superior to all outside the party (e.g., an uneducated party functionary in a university showing disdain for the non-party professors). The party leaders agreed that these vices had shown up in some areas, but they were not persuaded that any mass campaign was called for to rectify them.

Whether or not Mao was convinced that the intelligentsia had been won over, he did believe that party 'sectarianism' had alienated the intellectuals and that the party's work style with the intelligentsia needed to be rectified. In May 1956, Mao announced a new policy of 'Let a hundred flowers blossom, let a hundred schools of thought contend'. The speech in which he introduced this policy was not published, but the thrust of Mao's approach can be gauged from a report on the same subject made a short time later by Lu Dingyi, the director of the Propaganda Department and a recognized Maoist. The policy, ostensibly designed to give the intellectuals better working conditions and a restricted freedom to speak their minds ('bloom and contend'), also appeared to raise the status of the intelligentsia *vis-á-vis* the party. 'It is time for party members to take note of their own inadequacies and remedy them,' Lu said. 'There is only one way to do so: to seek advice and learn honestly and modestly from (the intellectuals) who know.' Though not categorically spelled out, the statement implied that the 'intellectuals' had the right to criticize the party.

Lu made it clear, however, that the new freedom was not granted to counterrevolutionaries and that it continued to limit artists and writers to produce works that 'serve the workers, peasants and soldiers'; therefore, 'it stands to reason that we must praise the new society and positive people . . . (and) criticize the old society and negative elements'.

1956 passed without the party or the intellectuals responding to Mao's calls for rectification or 'blooming and contending'.

Mao Zedong Takes Charge

Early in 1957 Mao launched a much more vigorous campaign for the rectification of the party work style with a speech entitled, 'On the Correct Handling of Contradictions Among the People', in which he combined a new thesis on classes and class conflict with a fresh analysis of the Hundred Flowers policy. Mao had written and spoken about 'contradictions' many times before, but what he did in February 1957 was to re-work his old concept and fit it into the contemporary political conditions. Mao explained that there were two types of contradictions: 'antagonistic contradictions' between ourselves and the enemy which could only be resolved through violence and the physical elimination of the enemy; and 'non-antagonistic contradictions' among ourselves which allowed for resolution through debate, education and persuasion.

Since the transition to socialism had followed the annihilation of class enemies, antagonistic contradictions had largely disappeared, although, Mao warned, a small number of counterrevolutionaries still existed. On the other hand, non-antagonistic contradictions (between the interest of the state and the interest of the individual, between the leaders and the masses, between party cadres and non-party officials, between the worker and management, and so on) existed everywhere and would continue to do so throughout the future. Contradictions created rifts and thwarted the realization of unity; therefore, they needed to be resolved. The process of resolution would not only bring unity, but raise society to a higher level; the process would be endless and ensure that society would keep improving itself ceaselessly, because new contradictions would inevitably arise, in due course, out of the new unity. Since the resolution of contradictions could only come through 'struggle' (criticism and debate), Mao reintroduced his old formula: 'unity–criticism–unity'.

In his speech Mao laid special emphasis on the contradictions between the leaders and the masses, pointing out that these contradictions were mainly due to the rise of bureaucratism in the work style of the leaders. Mao's speech, given in February, was not published till June, but as reported in the press in April, Mao had warned: 'Some leaders do not themselves understand conditions in the lower levels, and will not listen to the views of the masses . . . . There are even instances of the use of crude methods to suppress the views and demands of the masses, to undermine the rights and interests of the masses . . . . Many of our leaders have taken up the old practice of "once authority has been grasped, orders will be issued", and they simply rely on administrative orders to replace ideological and political work among the masses.'

Mao had used the widespread discontent among the masses (including the intellectuals) to stand forth as the true leader of all the people and attack the party chiefs who followed the Soviet model. In his 'contradictions' speech, Mao made a bold departure from previous policies and invited the intellectuals in all fields of activity to criticize the party for its shortcomings. Intellectuals belonging to non-communist parties, such as the Democratic League, which had been allowed to maintain a hollow existence after 1949, were told by Mao that he foresaw 'a long-term co-existence and *mutual supervision*' of political parties. Thus, the campaign for the rectification of the party and the Hundred Flowers campaign were merged.

There is reason to believe that there was considerable opposition to Mao within the party and many were afraid of throwing the party open to public criticism. However, since inner-party debates were never disclosed, all that can be said is that Mao obviously did manage to win the majority to his side and forced the party to launch a 'campaign of rectification of its work methods' on 27 April 1957.

The First Revolt of the Intellectuals: 'The Spring of 1957'

After some hesitation, and after the party had given repeated assurances that the critics had nothing to fear, the intellectuals began to raise their voices. For example, in a speech, Dr Lo Longji (Ph.D., Columbia University), the vice-chairman of the Democratic League, touched upon the question of proper jobs for the intellectuals. 'There are students who have returned after an education in Britain who make a living pulling carts, and there are students who have come back from the United States who sell cigarettes from street stalls.' Lo accused party cadres of humiliating the intellectuals (schoolteachers, for example, were ordered to do menial jobs). Referring to the traditional scholars' commitment to work for the benefit of the state, Lo suggested that their modern counterparts, given proper treatment, could also be drawn upon to become a vital part of the nation-building process. In the larger context of 'mutual supervision', leaders of the 'democratic parties' asserted that since they had been denied the right to freely recruit new members and since they were expected to strengthen the CCP leadership, they could have no programme of their own. Their existence was a farce. In the absence of any properly defined distinction between the CCP and the state, and in the absence of a legal system that could protect the citizens, the actions of party cadres were often arbitrary and unjust.

Many nationally renowned academic figures aired their own grievances and revealed through articles and speeches an intensity of discontent which few could have imagined. They deplored the conditions under which they worked and condemned the restraints placed on them by doctrinaire party cadres, who forced the academics to accept outmoded Soviet social science theories and irrationally punished the teachers who happened to disagree with them. The teachers asked why they were forbidden from teaching certain subjects just because they were not taught in the Soviet Union, and why they were not permitted to study scientific developments in Western capitalist countries which were ahead of the Soviet Union in many fields. The half-educated communist administrators in the institutions of higher learning had only one talent: they could make the professors tremble with fear. In short, the academicians questioned the competence of the party to guide intellectual activities.

When the students, the junior intellectuals, joined the campaign in May, the small trickle of mildly-worded criticism became a flood of vitriolic charges against the party. Millions of *da-zi-bao* (posters written in large Chinese characters) were posted on the walls of the campuses, and when there were no more bare walls left they were hung on strings stretched from tree to tree. The attacks went so far as to question the right of the CCP to govern the country ('China does not belong to the communist party alone'). The government was attacked for 'standing on the back of the masses', and there were suggestions that, if things did not change, there would be another revolution which would overthrow the party. In an article published in the *Chinese Youth Magazine*, a young writer talked of the economic conditions under the CCP:

> When pork is unavailable, it is difficult to convince the people that living standards have improved. Vegetable prices have increased by 600 per cent compared with the previous year. The common people have begun to lose confidence in the (CCP) and are saying that in some matters the situation is worse than it was in the days of the Kuomintang . . . . . The party will collapse soon.

Mao had hoped that the criticism would come as 'a gentle breeze' and had encouraged it with the slogan, 'Speak all you know and speak it fully; no fault will be attached to the speaker, while the listener will learn a lesson thereof'. Now, shocked by the volume and bitterness of the attacks, he brought the campaign to a sudden stop—hardly a month had passed since its official inauguration.

The action was justified on the basis of Mao's 'Contradictions' speech, which was finally published with many revisions in June. One section, obviously added, made a distinction between the blooming of 'fragrant flowers' and the sprouting of 'poisonous weeds' and gave several criteria to distinguish one from the other. Words, said Mao, should help to unite, not divide, the people; *be helpful, not harmful, to socialist construction*; help, not undermine, the people's democratic dictatorship and democratic centralism; and *they should strengthen, not shake-off or weaken, the leadership of the Communist Party*. According to the published speech,

Mao had the following to say about the intelligentsia:

> Among students and intellectuals there has recently been a falling off in ideological and political work, and some unhealthy tendencies have appeared. Some people seem to think that there is no longer any need to concern themselves with politics or with the future of the motherland and the ideals of mankind.... To counter these tendencies, we must strengthen our ideological and political work .... Not to have a correct political orientation is like not having a soul.

By revising his speech, Mao had ensured that the popular image of his boundless sagacity remained unimpaired. No one could censure him for being responsible for this explosion of discontent. It were the soul-less intellectuals who had produced stinking weeds and poisonous fruits—'rightists', who hankered after 'capitalism and the Western political system'. Mao now directed the party to quickly deal with these 'counterrevolutionaries' so that the gains of the socialist revolution were not lost. The rectification campaign was turned around 180 degrees: the critics, not the party, were to be rectified. An editorial in the *People's Daily on* 22 June, marked the beginning of the official counterattack:

> Some ask, 'Why does the party which invited others to rectify its working style, now rectify others?' True the party will continue to ask the broad masses of the people to help its rectification campaign .... But can it be said that the reactionary words and deeds of anti-socialist bourgeois rightists should be given protection and must not be criticized? If the revolutionary leaders of all circles do not know how to beware, detect and hit anti-socialist speeches and deeds (whatever sacred name they borrow), such revolutionaries simply have no sense of responsibility towards the people's cause.

By dubbing the critics 'bourgeois rightists', Mao had resurrected the 'antagonist' class enemy against whom state violence could be used. Since the critics, in fact, might not have a bourgeois class background (some, indeed, had risen from the ranks of the working classes), Mao had created an artificial condition for a supra-class struggle. Anybody with tainted thought was the enemy of the people. Deng Xiaoping, then the general secretary of the CCP, summed up the party's views on intellectuals with the strangely illogical statement:

> The intellectuals themselves do not constitute a class, since they belong to different classes. However, in the present situation of our country, most intellectuals do come from bourgeois and petty bourgeois family backgrounds . . . For the sake of convenience, they are, therefore, grouped together with the bourgeoisie.

How convenient!

Mao's conclusion that the actions of the intellectuals constituted a 'revolt' against the party was revealed in a speech by Lu Dingyi, the same party official who had first publicly revealed Mao's Hundred Flowers policy:

> The rightists actively disseminated ridiculous anti-socialist views. They attempted to seize the leadership of the democratic parties and among educationists, writers, artists, journalists, scientists, technicians, jurists, industrialists, and businessmen, as *a step prior to seizing leadership of the whole country*. They tried to provoke students to disturbances and judged that the 'student question' thus created had reached the point of explosion.

Even Zhou Enlai, who had shown some sympathy for the intelligentsia in 1956, came out strongly in favour of Mao's policy:

> (The) antagonist aspect of the contradiction between the bourgeoisie and the working class still exists at present and we still have a class struggle . . . (Therefore) we absolutely cannot ignore either the presence of class struggle or the contradictions between ourselves and the enemy. It is one of our important tasks to see that the fruits of the socialist revolution are made secure and that socialist transformation is carried forward to completion.

As late as 1958, when the party had already declared that the anti-rightist struggle had been successfully concluded, Zhou recommended that the struggle against the intellectuals be continued because 'the intellectuals are still harbouring in no small measure the consciousness and work style of capitalism'.

The 'anti-rightist' campaign became a massive, nationwide, vicious hunt for all persons who harboured 'bourgeois tendencies'. Teachers, journalists, writers, artists, engineers, doctors, technicians, managers of economic units, and party intellectuals (who had dared to express a dissident opinion or condoned the opinions of non-party intellectuals) were forced to go through thought-reform programmes, make grovelling public 'confessions' of their guilt and then dismissed from their posts (over half-a-million lost their jobs). A significant number committed suicide, while others were sent to the countryside to 'reform their thinking through labour'. Hundreds of thousands of students and teachers, whose thoughts were considered to be less tainted, were also 'sent down' to the countryside for a few months, during which period schools and colleges were closed down.

Lo Longji, mentioned earlier, like all the others who had been attacked, made a demeaning confession in which he practically declared that he was a counterrevolutionary. He ended his confession with the statement: 'My errors are serious, my guilt is grave. I am so ashamed of myself that I cannot find a hiding place. I have been untrue to Chairman Mao, to the leading party, to the . . . Democratic League, to the state and to the people of the nation . . . .'

Mao gloated over his achievement and was in no way displeased when he heard that the ruthless actions of the party had been compared to those of Qin Shi-huang-di (reigned: 221–208 BC). Shi-huang-di (First Emperor) was the Legalist ruler whose ascendance to power marks a major milestone in Chinese history because he effected the imperial unification of the country, which earlier had been divided into feudal states. The First Emperor has been praised by some traditional Chinese scholars for this outstanding achievement which required exceptional vision and courage, but also condemned by many others for establishing a most gruesomely barbaric and tyrannical government. On the advice of his Legalist chancellor, the emperor attempted to stamp out Confucian and other non-Legalist thought by 'burning books' and 'burying scholars alive'. Mao's reaction to the accusation that he was another Qin Shi-huang-di was:

> Ch'in (Qin) Shih-huang favoured the proposal that 'those who make use of the past to disparage the present should be exterminated with their whole families . . . . Ch'in Shih-huang did not amount to much. He only buried 460 Confucian scholars. We buried 46,000* of them . . . (We) have surpassed Ch'in Shih-huang a hundred times. If you denounce us for being Ch'in Shih-huang, for being autocrats, we admit everything.

The developments of 1957 saw Mao emerge as the unchallenged leader of the party. While the Hundred Flowers campaign had proved that the intellectuals were undependable and that the party would have to rely on the mass-based Maoist model for national development, the Anti-Rightist campaign had cleared the path for applying this model by eliminating, or silencing, Mao's opponents within the party.

* This is, obviously, an artificial figure meant to imply that a 'large number' were killed. The estimated number of intellectuals liquidated in the 'thought reform' programmes is 80,000; another 300,000 were found politically unreliable and deprived of their civil rights.

3

Mao Zedong's China: 1958–76 From Upheaval to Upheaval

Having gained near-absolute authority over the party in late 1957, Mao Zedong could begin experimenting with his model of national development. That China was facing immense economic problems was a fact: the population had crossed the 600,000,000 figure; unemployment was increasing; since Soviet aid had gone primarily to the building of heavy industry, the country was short of consumer goods; agricultural growth was not keeping pace with the demands of the industrial sector; and China could not depend on an increase in the Soviet aid commensurate with the needs of the Second Five-Year-Plan which was to commence in 1958. In brief, China on the one hand had a growing population that reduced the impact of economic growth, and on the other was short of investment funds and capital goods.

Mao and China's Manpower

From the very inception of the People's Republic, economists and planners, worried about the negative impact of the country's population growth, had tried to devise policies that encouraged some kind of family planning. The Marriage Law, introduced in 1950, had raised the marriage age for men to twenty and for women to eighteen, and it was hoped that this would not only reduce the productive years of the wife but that a maturer couple would not desire too many children.

The first census, carried out in 1953, revealed that the population had reached the startlingly high figure of 570,000,000. The government promptly legalized abortions and sterilizations, but it was only in March 1957, after years of inner party debate, that a formal birth-control campaign was launched with the declaration that the country was over-populated and that, 'if our population growth is not in accordance with planned child-birth, it will prevent our country from quickly ridding itself of poverty and from becoming prosperous and powerful'.

A birth-control campaign followed, and foreigners who were in China at that time were amazed at the methodical manner in which thousands of organized groups from neighbourhoods, factories and farms were brought to the exhibition halls to be shown how conception could be prevented by the use of contraceptives. Nothing was left to the imagination. Young women pulled stocking-sized contraceptives over huge models of the male organ and explained, to an embarrassed audience, how it all worked. Late marriages, spacing of children, and sterilization was also encouraged.

But, a few months later, in November, the campaign was halted with the suddenness which only China is capable of, and the people were told that China was short of manpower! This was a clear signal that Mao Zedong had managed to acquire the power and authority he needed to begin his experiment with the nation.

Mao firmly believed that production could be increased by harnessing the untapped energy of the people and that the masses, ideologically inspired and properly mobilized, could perform economic miracles which the experts could not even conceive of. As early as June, two months into the birth-control campaign, Mao had remarked: 'We have a population of six hundred million and this is our asset. We have this large population. It is a good thing . . .' According to Mao, labour was capital.

By following Mao's path, China could become 'self-reliant' and no longer would have to depend on Soviet, or any other, foreign aid. What the country needed was not more money or machinery but more people.

Mao proved his thesis by launching a mass construction work drive in the winter of 1957–58, after the peasants had brought in the autumn harvest and before they started their spring plowing. Mao's calculation was simple, but his vision was uniquely original and compellingly bold. Mao got the party cadres to whip up the enthusiasm of the peasantry through rudimentary ideology (they were the 'masters' of the land working for their own good) and inspire them with a vision of a prosperous tomorrow ('hard work for a few years, happiness for a thousand'). Millions of these peasants were then organized into work brigades and put to the task of digging canals and irrigation channels, raising dikes, building dams and laying down roads. At the end of the campaign, the country was told that during the normally idle winter season, the peasants, using no modern machinery and employing no modern technology, had (among other achievements) increased the irrigated acreage in the country by fifty-three million acres.

By the spring of 1958, party leaders who had expressed doubts about the feasibility of large collectives and mass mobilization, were forced by the socio-political environment created by Mao to go along with his schemes and endorse his policies. All ideas of a regulated and centrally controlled Soviet-style planning were set aside and replaced with the Maoist strategy of 'The Great Leap Forward' (GLF). The Second Five-Year-Plan had called for raising industrial production by fourteen to fifteen per cent a year, but the GLF aimed at raising it by 100 per cent in one year! In a parallel leap, grain production was to be doubled in 1958 and redoubled in 1959!

The Great Leap Forward
Mao's First Great Experiment With the Nation

The Great Leap Forward has sometimes come to be associated with Mao's quixotic attempt to achieve unrealistic economic goals. In fact, it was a design to transform every aspect of Chinese society, though the Marxist notion that economic development had to precede a change in the superstructure (human consciousness) did play some role in Mao's thinking.

Mao's premise was that the 'outstanding characteristic' of the 600 million Chinese people was that they were 'poor and blank'; therefore, they were desirous and ready for advancing the cause of the communist revolution. Although this notion itself is debatable, it does show how far Mao had gone in totally rejecting the Marxist idea that communism could only come to a highly advanced industrialized society. 'Poverty', wrote Mao, 'gives rise to the desire for change, the desire for action and the desire for revolution. On a blank sheet of paper free from any mark, the freshest and most beautiful characters can be written, the freshest and most beautiful pictures painted.'

This is an intriguing statement made by a person who had always spoken of the wisdom of the masses! Since only Mao knew what these beautiful characters were going to be, and what the beautiful paintings would look like, only he, in a god-like fashion, could direct the activities of the millions of his countrymen to bring about the grand transfiguration of the nation.

The GLF was to immediately, and simultaneously, fulfil many of the Maoist goals, such as a concurrent industrial development in the interior as well as the coastal cities, an integration of intellectual and physical labour, turning party members into 'red experts' (possessing both ideological understanding and knowledge of science and technology), and so forth. Mao declared that by exploiting the 'subjective initiative of the masses as a mighty driving force' the country would achieve 'greater, faster, better, and more economical results', and catch up with Britain in fifteen years. The watchword of the GLF was 'uninterrupted revolution'—one revolutionary task following another so that there was no pause in between for the people to become content or apathetic.

By its very nature, the GLF could not be based on any carefully worked out blueprint for action, and several campaigns were launched one after the other to tackle problems as they arose. However, at the high point of the Leap one could see how Mao's general instructions meshed together and provided a vision of the 'good society' he was trying to create. Not surprisingly, it was the peasantry that led Mao's GLF revolution, and the 'new socialist man' first appeared in the countryside.

The fundamental demand of the GLF was that all able-bodied citizens, wherever they were and whatever their calling, discard all narrow, selfish, individualistic desires for personal gain and exert their utmost effort with only one goal in mind: to make the motherland rich and prosperous. This meant that all ideas of so-called 'normal' working life were given up. Workers in the factories extended their working hours to the point of exhaustion; city women, not employed in production units, devised ways and means to set up neighbourhood workshops to produce ancillary goods; peasants not only worked zealously to increase grain production by 'close planting and deep plowing', but found time to set up 'backyard furnaces' and produce pig iron; the millions of intellectuals, bureaucrats and managers, sent down to the countryside in the anti-rightist campaign, helped the overworked peasants in their multifarious jobs. Nobody was idle. Even the artists and writers 'leapt forward' by declaring unbelievably high targets of how many poems, or novels, or paintings they would produce in the coming year.

The involvement of the peasants in non-agricultural activity did, indeed, lead to a shortage of manpower, and peasant women had to be drafted to join their men to work in the fields and in making iron; apart from building dams and other waterworks, the peasants had set up 600,000 backyard furnaces across the country to manufacture pig iron. Since the time spent by the peasants in tending to their children and cooking meals was considered counterproductive, the party encouraged them to establish communal mess halls and nurseries. This logically led to the next step: the disbandment of the cooperatives and the establishment of 'people's communes' in which all land and property was collectivized; the peasants no longer had any private agricultural plots to worry over, or privately-owned pigs and chickens to divert them from the communal tasks enjoined by the GLF. Some communes housed men and women in separate dormitories; couples were assigned time and place where they could meet periodically, and lactating mothers were allowed to go to the nurseries, at fixed hours, to breast-feed their babies.

In August 1958 the party made the establishment of communes official policy, and by November China's 750,000 cooperatives (average membership: 160 families) were amalgamated into 26,578 communes (average membership: 4,600 families), which became the basic unit of local government with functions that included farming, industry, commerce, and education.

For even more efficient exploitation of peasant muscle-power, an 'Everyone a Soldier Movement' was started in late 1958. Though the declared intention was to produce a People's Militia, a fighting force for the defence of the country, the movement was actually aimed at creating collective discipline and raising 'shock troops of production under military discipline'. Labour units were now organized into platoons, battalions, and brigades. The militarized units lived in their individual dormitories, rose in the morning with reveille, marched to work to the beat of drums, and retired from work with bugle calls.

All these bizarre developments were taken as evidence by Mao that China had moved ahead of the Soviet Union. China now had a socialist egalitarian society, albeit in the countryside, where the peasants had been transformed into 'workers'. They were engaged in both agricultural and 'industrial' activities (besides steel-making the peasants had also set up small machine-tool and repair shops) and recompensed through a wage system. Some communes went so far as to do away with money as a medium of exchange and to experiment with the free supply of food and other basic commodities. The traditional pattern of human relations, built on the basis of the family unit and the selfish familial bonds that it represented, had been shattered and all loyalty was now focussed on the state and the party. Human nature had been transformed. People were no longer motivated by material incentives but by the desire to selflessly work for the common good. China was clearly on the threshold of establishing the first 'perfectly non-exploitative system mankind has ever known'.

Ostensibly, Mao Zedong had also succeeded in carrying out a technological revolution along with the economic and ideological revolution. According to Mao, the myth that science and technology were some kind of 'mystery' that the common people could not acquire was created by bourgeois intellectuals, and the myth could be demolished because 'technology' was no more than 'the summation of labour in action'. Could the semi-literate masses and the half-educated party members actually produce 'red intellectuals' who could displace the abhorrent bourgeois intellectuals? 'Yes', said Mao.

> Ever since ancient times the people who have founded new schools of thought were all young people without too much learning . . . . The old fogies with learning always opposed them . . . I am told that penicillin was invented by a man who worked as a laundryman in a dyers and cleaners (one wonders how Sir Alexander Fleming would have reacted to that state-

ment!) .... *What I mean to say is that it is not absolutely necessary to attend school.*

The Leap supposedly proved Mao right and helped to produce an impressive number of 'technologists' and 'scientists' from among the masses. This could be viewed as the first step in the formation of an 'army of red experts' which Mao was hoping to create to replace the bourgeois intellectuals.

Since the bourgeois intellectuals were of two kinds, those in arts and literature (the humanities) and those in the sciences, Mao decided that the peasants must reveal their latent talent in both these fields. A poetry 'writing' (the word is incorrectly used because most peasants were totally illiterate and could not 'write') campaign was started, and a flood of poetry gushed forth from the countryside. To take one example, 300,000 peasants in 'creative groups' in Jiangsu province were reported to have produced 10,000,000 items within six months. The poems generally eulogized Mao and spoke of the abundance of harvests that made the happy peasants sing and dance. The bourgeois intellectuals who had been sent down to the villages to 'learn from the peasants' collected the poetry for posterity. The following are three examples of the kind of poems that were being written:

(1) Everyone eats full without pay
Our ancestors never heard of it!
Is it a dream?
No, it's a fact!
Where?
Right here!
The east is red!
Hail to Mao Zedong!

(2) Sugar is sweet but honey sweeter,
Cotton is warm but fur warmer.
Mother and father have loving kindness,
But Chairman Mao has more.

(3) We work at such white heat,
If we bump the sky it will break,
If we kick the earth it will crack.
If the sky falls our commune will mend it.
If the earth splits our commune will patch it.

There was a similar upsurge of 'scientific activity' in the countryside. 'Inventors' and 'technicians' began to devise tools and locally produce much-needed equipment which the cities were not supplying. At a higher plane, 'scientists' like Li Shimei, emerged; Li, who had 'only a few years of schooling', discovered a highly successful system of exterminating termites. Li's discovery was so important that he was invited by many universities to talk about his findings. In mid-1958 he was appointed a professor in the Zhongshan University.

In July 1958 the party organ *Hong-qi* (Red Flag) clarified the use of the term 'scientist' as applied to the peasant experts:

> Somehow we feel that a scientist must be one who has been to a university, spent long time in the laboratory experimenting, has books to his credit, and is a higher intellectual with grey hair. Wang Baojing (a peasant expert) has been only two years in a primary school, he is a young man who has not even written a single article. Under no circumstances can we link such a man with the designation 'scientist'. But now we realize that this is so because we have made a 'mystery' of the word 'scientist'. This is superstition. Wang is a scientist in name and in fact. He is the new type of scientist who has been fostered by our party.

Inspired by Mao's ideals, the Chinese educational system was revolutionized so that it could better serve the cause of the socialist revolution currently underway. The goal of the change was to destroy the 'bourgeois' viewpoints which divorced education from politics and labour, put vocational expertise above 'redness', and fostered individualism through competitive examinations. To eliminate the difference between intellectual and physical labour, schools were encouraged to invite experienced peasants and workers to establish farms and factories in the schools, where students could labour physically and learn from the masses. Similarly, communes and factories opened spare-time schools for peasants and workers. 'With the schools operating factories, farms, and other social undertakings on a large scale and teachers and students participating in productive labour and in practical work, knowledge was greatly enriched, and wisdom was cultivated . . . . The method of recruiting locally men of ability to serve as teachers was adopted to solve the problem of teaching staff . . . (and in a few months) there were set up in different places throughout the country several hundred thousand workers' and peasants' schools of all grades and patterns'.

The party's faith in Mao's view of knowledge can be judged from Liu Shaoqi's advice to his granddaughter, discouraging her from going to college: 'Neither chairman Mao nor I have never been to college. But we are not inferior to those who have been to college. Knowledge in the world stems from two sources: natural science and social science. And this can be acquired in actual work of training.'

The Shattering of Mao's Dream: The Outcome of the Leap

As the year 1958 came to a close, it became apparent that Mao Zedong's multi-pronged revolution to reshape the Chinese nation had failed.

The nation was exhausted but had little to show for its efforts. The claims of the GLF of record outputs were proven to be figments of the enthusiastic cadres' imagination. This should have come as no surprise because Mao had often said that there was no harm in falsifying statistics if it helped to inspire the masses. The masses had been inspired, but now Mao had to face the consequences of his misguided approach. The biggest shock came when it was realized that in some areas peasants were starving because of food shortages.

According to the GLF figures the production of cereals had risen from 196 million tons in 1957 to 375 million tons in 1958. The actual increase was only thirty-three million tons, and even though this was in itself a fair achievement, famine and food shortages hit certain districts because of a variety of reasons: the peasants in some localities had concentrated on growing non-cereal crops and because of the breakdown in the distribution system, food could not be rushed to them; the crops were abundant but there was no male 'muscle-power' available to harvest them—the men were working in the backyard furnaces or in local industries. In some communes the bumper crops had been hastily divided among the peasants, and little was left for state procurement. Marshal Peng Dehuai, the defence minister, was so moved by the wretched plight of the peasantry in one area which he inspected that he wrote a touching poem:

> Millet is scattered all over the ground,
> The leaves of the sweet potatoes are withered.
> The young and the strong have gone to smelt iron,
> To harvest the grain there are children and old women.
> How shall we get through next year?
> I shall agitate and speak on behalf of the people.*

In many areas the situation worsened when the rains came and washed away the thin layer of top soil which had been loosened by 'deep plowing', or demolished the dams and dikes which had been built without any calculation of future water pressure.

Similarly the claim that industry had grown by seventy per cent had to be scaled down to 39.3 per cent. Here, too, the very respectable figure of 39.3 per cent hid an ocean of troubles. Three million tons of backyard steel, produced by peasants who had spent sleepless nights, was found unusable. Hundreds of thousands of machines, machinery parts, electric motors, and tools had to be discarded because of sloppy workmanship. Heavy machinery, which had been used to produce these items, began to break down because it had been overworked and not properly maintained. Thousands of tons of manufactured articles, overproduced by enthusiastic workers without regard to demand, lay stored in the open, rusting and decaying.

The zeal which had marked the high tide of the GLF in mid-year began to give way to disillusionment and frustration. Peasants, exhausted and

* See Roderick MacFarquhar, *The Origins of the Cultural Revolution*, Vol. 2, New York: Columbia University Press, 1983, p. 200.

worn out from a year of inordinately hard labour ('shock production brigades' worked two days and two nights at a stretch and were back to work after a twelve-hour rest), found that life was no better than it was before. In fact, it had worsened in many cases. The compulsory establishment of communes also brought widespread fear that the party was out to destroy family life and take away the peasant's private possessions.

As reality ripped away the curtain of self-deception, the 'Pragmatists' (sometimes referred to as 'conservatives') in the party gained an opportunity to air their anxieties and appeal for a slowdown in the tempo of the GLF and in Mao's push for full communism. Their cause was helped by the problems created by famines and floods (largely a consequence of the GLF) and the growing antagonism of the peasantry to life in the communes. In its meeting in December 1958, the Central Committee of the party set down certain guidelines for the cadres to pacify the peasant masses and ordered the cadres to publicize the following decisions of the party:

1. The communes will not dispossess the peasants of their privately owned property (housing, clothing, bedding, furniture, and bank deposits).

2. Peasants could continue to engage in domestic side occupations and retain the trees around their houses, their pigs and poultry, and their tools.

3. The 'military work style' will be discarded and peasants will be guaranteed eight hours for sleep and four hours for meals; women will be allowed a period of rest before and after delivery and during menstruation.

4. Certain commune members may be allowed to cook at home (this soon became the general rule); parents could withdraw their children from communal nurseries (which soon became the general practice).

5. Peasants will be paid cash wages.

The GLF was not immediately abandoned, but Mao Zedong was forced to accept a temporary retreat. The three calamitous years that followed made Mao's vision even more untenable and there was a further shift away from his leftist policies. But before the long-term consequences of the GLF are discussed, it is proper to ask: How could Mao have gained such a free hand to experiment with a nation of 650,000,000?

The Roots of Mao's Dictatorial Power

There were at least four reasons for the inordinate power that Mao came to wield. First was his role as the charismatic leader of the Chinese revolution. There were, no doubt, other leaders who had played a significant role in the making of the revolution, but it was universally recognized that Mao was the key figure who had brought the revolution to a successful conclusion.

Mao, himself, appears to have believed that he alone had all the answers to China's problems and that the masses had absolute faith in him; this had nothing to do with his association with the communist party, but was a reflection of his personal popularity. Perhaps this view of Mao was best revealed in 1959, when Peng Dehuai criticized Mao's GLF policies at a party meeting. The criticism was relatively mild and discreetly directed both at Mao and the party as a whole. Mao Zedong, the great proponent of 'criticism' and 'self-criticism' should have accepted it in the spirit it had been offered. But Mao, like the emperors in imperial China, considered himself above criticism and angrily responded that if the party had made so many mistakes it deserved to perish:

> In that case, I will go to the countryside to lead the peasants to overthrow the government. If those of you in the Liberation Army won't follow me, then I will go and found a Red Army, and organize another Liberation Army.

No party leader, other than Mao, could have been dreamt of making such an audacious statement.

The second source of Mao's power was the Chinese Communist Party (CCP). Mao, as the principal ideologist and organizer of the party whose guidance (according to its Constitution) was provided by 'Marxism–Leninism Thought of Mao Zedong', was looked to by common party members as 'The Supreme Leader'. His leading position within the party was guaranteed by his life term as chairman of the CCP. Structurally, the CCP was controlled by a small core of leaders, Mao being one of them, who formed the Standing Committee of the Politburo (seven in number in 1959). As long as Mao commanded a majority in the Standing Committee he could have his policies approved with comparative ease. Whenever, for tactical reasons, Mao felt it necessary, he added loyal members to the Committee, or purged recalcitrant ones. And if there was a general consensus against any of his policies, as was the case in 1957, Mao did not hesitate to short-circuit the Standing Committee of the Politburo and take his case directly to the provincial party secretaries. Since policy conflicts and debates within the Politburo were never made public, Mao's image as chief architect of party policies remained untarnished.

Third, Mao strengthened his position by fostering a cult of personality that exalted him above all mankind. During the year of the Leap the myth-makers deified Mao to such an extent that every word spoken by him was received with awe. Mao was likened to the sun that provides light and life wherever it shines. He was glorified as 'The Great Helmsman' who alone could guide the ship of state through perilous, unchartered seas to utopia. Mao was a prophet whose 'every prophesy had become a reality'. A song popularized during the GLF proclaimed, 'The east is red. The sun rises. China has brought forth a Mao Zedong! He toils for the people's happiness. He is the people's great saviour.' Mao's portraits were hung in every home and every office, and when the campaign 'Give Your Heart to the Party' was launched in 1958, people of all ages and from all walks of life were organized to stand before a portrait of Mao, put their hands on their hearts and swear allegiance to him. Never has a leader, not even Stalin, been so idolized in his own lifetime. Speaking at a meeting held in 1958, in honour of the thirty-seventh anniversary of CCP, Chen Boda, a leading Maoist ideologue acclaimed Mao's contribution to China in the following words:

> It is under the great banner of Comrade Mao Zedong that the Chinese people are forging ahead.
>
> Mao Zedong's banner is a banner of combining the Chinese Communists and the people, a banner integrating the universal truth of Marxism–Leninism with the concrete practice of the Chinese revolution, and a banner of creatively applying Marxism–Leninism under the conditions of China. Therefore, Mao Zedong's banner is a banner of victory of the Chinese people's revolution

and socialist construction.

> Mao Zedong's banner is a red flag held aloft by the Chinese people. Guided by this great red flag *the Chinese people will in the not distant future enter the great Communist society.*

Lastly, and not least importantly, the authority/obedience syndrome that characterized Chinese traditional political culture reinforced Mao's unassailable position. The Chinese masses, trained through two thousand years of imperial China to accept authority without questioning it and to worship the semi-divine emperor as the provider of shelter and livelihood, were psychologically prepared to revere Mao as their 'father-mother' ruler. In keeping with the long historical tradition, the Chinese people lived up to the expectation that they would docilely, and with apparent enthusiasm, uphold and execute all the pre-determined policies without question.

For these many reasons, in 1958 Mao acquired the kind of absolute authority exercised by Qin Shi-huang-di. Normally one would have expected state structures to intervene between him and the masses, but the institutions of the state lacked constitutional authority and were entwined with the party hierarchy which wielded all the power. Besides, Mao's penchant for government by upheaval kept state institutions from taking firm root.

Also, the intelligentsia that could have (and did) opposed Mao, had been eliminated from the political scene. So, like the Qin emperor, who in the third century BC had ordered millions of peasants to build the Great Wall, Mao, two thousand years later, mobilized ten million peasants to make steel in their backyard furnaces. But while the Great Wall did have some utility, the backyard steel proved to be a colossal waste of human effort. Is it possible to imagine any leader in India capable of exercising such control over the masses?

At this juncture it is pertinent to reiterate that Mao's 'dictatorship' was not based on the use of terror *per se*, but was a product of the unique Chinese political culture described above. It is important to remember that though Mao was the principal actor in the GLF, other key leaders of the party accepted his leadership and joined him in supporting his campaign. For example, Liu Shaoqi and Deng Xiaoping, who would later surface as the chief opponents of Maoism, made innumerable strongly-worded speeches supporting the Leap. It should also not be forgotten that, in the beginning at least, the masses also displayed a sincere enthusiasm for the campaign.

The Two line Struggle: 1959–65
Retreat from Maoism

The tragedy of the Great Leap Forward did not lead to the fall of Mao Zedong, but Mao, however reluctantly, had to allow the Pragmatists to come forth and repair the damaged economy. Unfortunately for the nation, severe natural calamities hit China during the next three years and exacerbated the situation. Widespread floods and droughts brought hunger and malnutrition to millions and compelled China to import food grains. To add to China's troubles, the growing dispute between Beijing and Moscow also came to a head in 1960 when the Soviet Union abruptly terminated its economic assistance programme and withdrew all the Russian specialists helping in Chinese industrial projects. The industrial output fell drastically.

Agricultural output value in 1959 was less than that in 1957, and in 1960 and 1961 it was below that in 1952. The mortality rate increased dramatically when nearly twenty-five million people died of starvation or malnutrition-related causes. These figures cannot even remotely convey the anguish and misery of the people living in the afflicted areas where peasants were driven to eat grass, wild plants, tree bark and leaves. The cities were slightly better off because of imported grain, but they lacked meat and vegetables.

An interesting article on Mao's relations with his children, published in the 18–24 September 1989 issue of Beijing Review, recalls the food situation in Beijing in 1960. Though the article, published twenty-nine years after the event, is intended to show that Mao, unlike the corrupt leaders of today, opposed privileges and shared the misfortune of the masses, it does help us to gain a glimpse of the horrendous winter of 1960. The article informs us that Mao's nineteen-year-old daughter Li Na came home from school one weekend and complained to her father,

'My ration is not enough. Just vegetables boiled in water. My stomach often rumbles in class.' That evening when dinner was served Li Na 'sniffed her bowl of red unpolished rice and sweet potato'. 'How delicious!' she said. Li Na did not realize that this dinner had been made specially for her; 'If she had known that sometimes (Mao) only had purslane, a herb cooked as a vegetable, for a meal, she would not have eaten so much and so quickly.'

> 'Today's dinner is so delicious, but . . .' She cast a sidelong glance at her father. With childish cunning, she said to the guard, 'Is there any hot water? I want to wash the plates and drink it so that there is no waste.'
>
> With tears in his eyes, the guard rushed to the kitchen. The cook gave him two pieces of steamed bread made with flour from wheat and corn.
>
> Li Na looked at her father, a little ill at ease. She broke a piece of bread, cleaned a plate with it and then put it into her mouth. The guard fetched some hot water and helped Li Na to wash the plates and then she drank the water.

If a special dinner served at Mao's residence consisted of 'red unpolished rice' (the poorest quality rice), bread made of the horrifying combination of wheat and corn, and sweet potatoes (instead of meat), one can imagine what the peasants in the interior were eating!

The troubled years, naturally, led to a sense of demoralization among the peasants. The disheartened communist cadres at the commune level could not be expected to continue to mobilize the peasants seething with resentment, or to insist on their following the rigorous practices imposed by the party during 1958. The peasants began to drift into old habits and search out ways and means to gain material profits. They began to neglect work on the communal fields and devote as much time as they could on 'sideline occupations', such as raising livestock and growing vegetables on the 'private plots', produce items which brought good, ready cash in the thriving black markets that sprang up spontaneously in food-scarce cities and towns.

The Pragmatists in Power

At the end of 1958, just about the time the party set out new guidelines for the communes (which marked a retreat from the GLF goals), Mao Zedong announced that he would resign as chairman of the Republic in 1959 and that Liu Shaoqi would take over the post. It is not necessary for our purposes to discuss the various theories concerning his resignation; suffice it to say that his departure gave an opportunity to the Pragmatists, led by Liu Shaoqi, to gradually entrench themselves in power during the next seven years. Mao remained chairman of the party and the Pragmatists continued to pay lip service to him while discreetly shifting away from his mass-based policies. Thus, while Mao's public image remained unsullied, some in the party hierarchy began to subtly criticize Mao's idealistic but impractical policies. As will be discussed later, Mao tried very hard to keep the party from deviating from the principles he had laid down, but to no avail. Finally, in a desperate move, Mao used his immense popular prestige to make a comeback and launch his next 'revolution', the Great Proletarian Cultural Revolution, in 1966.

The split between the 'two lines', the radical left line of Mao Zedong and the pragmatic line identified with Liu Shaoqi, first became public in mid-1959 at a meeting of the Politburo where Marshal Peng Dehuai criticized Mao's GLF policies. As has been mentioned earlier, Mao took this criticism to be a personal attack and instead of debating the issues made it a matter of honour that party chiefs declare their allegiance to him. Because of Mao's immense prestige nobody dared to come to the support of Peng, who was dismissed for heading a rightist 'anti-party' clique and replaced as minister of defence by the Maoist general Lin Biao. The Pragmatists were taken aback by Mao's tactics and though they had sacrificed Peng for practical reasons, they were not convinced by Mao's logic.

Broadly speaking, after Mao had withdrawn from the front line, the Pragmatists took steps to strengthen the party apparatus so that the party could re-exert its centralized control over the country. They increased investment allocated to agriculture, re-centralized industry, shifted emphasis away from inefficient small local production units to large 'modern' factories and plants, brought back the experts to help in planning and managing the economy, re-emphasized quality in education and devalued the unorthodox 'half-work, half-study' schools run by semi-educated cadres and popularized by Mao during the GLF.

The Pragmatists decentralized the communes and gave power to 'production teams' (composed of twenty to thirty families) to determine how they wanted to utilize their land allocation and how they would distribute their profits. In return the production teams had to guarantee the state a certain fixed amount of agricultural produce—an amount far less than that demanded in 1958–59. Private plots, taken away in 1958, were returned to peasant households in 1961, and the peasants officially allowed to pursue their side-line activities and freely sell their produce in rural and urban 'black markets' ('black' because the prices charged were much higher than those fixed by the government for the same items). These material incentives worked wonders, and agricultural production began to rise dramatically from 1962 on. Deng Xiaoping, the secretary general of the party, later condemned by the Maoists as the 'second most important capitalist-roader in the party', proudly declared: 'Private farming is all right as long as it raises production, just as it doesn't matter whether a cat is black or white as long as it catches mice.'

In effect, these policies meant that communes, as envisaged by Mao, had disappeared. Instead of being self-sufficient, practically autonomous, self-governing units, the communes were now reduced to administering public works and security organs. Even the size of the communes was reduced to less than half. Communal mess halls, children's nurseries, and old people's homes disappeared, and old-style family units re-emerged.

Industrial recovery was even more rapid. The Leap targets were pushed down to more realistic levels; with proper planning and the utilization of technical and managerial skills, impressive gains were made in many fields of industrial development. Never mind that the party had to bring back the old 'rightist' economists, engineers, scientists, capitalists and businessmen to restore order in the industrial field. It goes to the credit of the indigenous Chinese expertise that industrial output grew at the remarkable rate of twenty-seven per cent a year for light industry, and seventeen per cent a year for heavy industry from 1963 to 1965.

The need for 'expertness' naturally meant a decline of emphasis on 'redness' and more liberal policies towards the intelligentsia. The party removed the label of 'rightist' from students and teachers who had been so branded during 1958 for either their activities in the Hundred Flowers campaign or for their class origin. There were also signs that elements of the pre-GLF educational system, which accented quality, competitiveness and individual achievement, were being silently restored.

This retreat from Mao's overwhelming emphasis on 'redness' was perhaps best expressed by foreign minister Chen Yi in a speech delivered at Beijing University in 1961. Chen Yi said that socialist construction needed all kinds of experts and that an expert working for socialist construction was automatically serving the cause of politics. It was, therefore, 'wrong for ordinary schools to allot so much time to political studies and labour that they have to loosen their grip on specialized studies'. Were this course to be followed 'our country will always remain backward scientifically and culturally'. He then asked his audience a rhetorical question: what good is a 'red' pilot to the defence of the motherland if he does not have the proper expertise to fly his plane? Chen Yi also made a remarkable statement concerning the question of 'individualism':

> Take myself for instance. My mind is a complicated one. I have communist thoughts, thoughts of the school of Confucius, thoughts of the school of Mencius, *and even bourgeois thoughts*. I have been in the revolution for 40 years, but I still cannot say that I am 'thoroughly red' . . . . Hence, it is a non-Marxist-Leninist practice to deal with the ideological problems of a young student simply by threatening him with disciplinary action, or try to have ideological problems of young students solved by means of some criticism.

Following Chen Yi's speech the party took further action to rehabilitate professors who had been labelled 'rightists', re-open fields of pure research which had been condemned for lacking a vital connection with the daily life of the masses, and relax controls on the work of writers and artists.

Many party intellectuals who had been genuinely troubled by the dislocation caused by the GLF began to evaluate the causes and failures of the upheaval. Their analysis inevitably led them to a critical view of Mao's romantic faith in the will power of the masses to overcome all economic and political limitations. They were also disturbed by the 'despotic' manner in which Mao had dismissed Peng Dehuai. Some of the establishment intellectuals, protected by pragmatist patrons, had the temerity to write essays, stories, and plays in which they, by analogy and indirection, attacked the Great Helmsman himself!

Wu Han, the deputy mayor of Beijing was one such intellectual. Born in 1909 to a middle class family, Wu received a university education and was trained as a Ming historian by some of China's most eminent scholars. He became a teacher after graduation, and his scholarly writings brought him national distinction and fame. Disillusioned by Nationalist policies, Wu Han joined the communist movement in 1948. After Liberation he was made deputy mayor of Beijing and given other assignments connected with the fields of education and culture. Wu Han was accepted as member of the CCP in 1957.

In 1959, Wu Han published a piece in the *People's Daily* on Hai Rui, an upright, incorruptible Ming official who had championed the cause of the 'masses' and upbraided the emperor for levying exorbitantly heavy taxes. Mao approved of the article. Wu Han was later asked to turn the subject of Hai Rui into a play, which he did. The play was published in 1960 under the title, *Hai Rui Dismissed From Office*. The play deals with a peasant family that has been grievously abused by its oppressive landlord (who had once served as a high official) and his dissolute son. The landlord seizes the peasant's land, which drives the poor man to his death. The son then kidnaps the peasant's beautiful daughter and beats up her grandfather when the latter comes to her rescue. The girl's mother and grandfather complain to the magistrate, but the magistrate, who had been bribed by the landlord's son, instead of helping the persecuted peasant family, has the grandfather flogged to death. Just about this time, Hai Rui happens to be appointed to the district. As soon as he learns of the peasants' problems, he passes orders that the landlord's son be executed and the landlord return all illegally confiscated lands to the peasants. Hai Rui performs these acts knowing fully well that the landlord will use his old connections in the bureaucracy to get Hai Rui dismissed.

The play which, on the surface, has an innocuous theme based on historically verifiable facts, came to be viewed by the Maoists, and Mao himself, as a satirical attack on the Great Leader. In 1965, four years after the publication of the play and its first performance, Wu Han was vehemently criticized for 'using the past to satirize the present'. According to the critics, the emperor stood for Mao, Hai Rui for Peng Dehuai; Hai Rui's dismissal by a despotic emperor was analogous to Peng's dismissal by Mao; Hai Rui's 'returning of the land' was Peng's criticism of the commune system and his plea that the excesses of collectivization be reversed and peasants given back some of their land (private plots). As we shall see later in the chapter, it was the attack on Wu Han that signalled the beginning of the Great Proletarian Cultural Revolution which overthrew the Pragmatists and brought Mao back to power.

Whether or not Wu Han had intentionally written the play to make a veiled criticism of Mao became an irrelevant issue because the Maoists decided that it was so. There were, indeed, many party intellectuals who were busy writing satirical essays in which they deliberately used historical examples and oblique allusions to condemn the errors of the GLF and the policies of Mao Zedong. One of them, Deng Tuo (born 1912; party member since 1930), a long time editor of the *People's Daily*, was perhaps the most outspoken. He chose famous historical figures (as analogues for Mao) whom he could attack for 'lacking humility' and for 'asserting their own unrealistic ideas without consulting others'. He went so far as to suggest that Mao was mentally ill and needed to go on a long holiday. The angered Maoists, naturally, wanted to get rid of these 'poisonous weeds', and Wu Han happened to provide them a most convenient target.

Mao Zedong's Counterattack

Mao Zedong, to say the least, was not happy with the way politics were unfolding in the post-Leap era.

Since 1958, even before his retirement from the chairmanship of the People's Republic, Mao had ceased to participate in the Politburo meetings, and this had given the Pragmatists a freer hand in policy-making.

The Pragmatists continued to treat Mao with respect and pay lip-service to his ideology, but felt little need to confer with him or take his periodic directions too seriously. That Mao had resented this behaviour was revealed years later in a remark he made that persons like Deng Xiaoping had stopped consulting him altogether and that his adversaries treated him like a 'dead ancestor' (you pay homage to a dead ancestor but do not have to worry about his giving you any advice).

Although Mao had lost control of the party, he was in no way totally inactive. Mao continued to guide foreign relations and remained the principal architect of China's foreign policy. In his capacity as chairman of the Military Affairs Commission, he also retained a firm control over the People's Liberation Army. Here he was greatly helped by the defence minister Lin Biao, a committed Maoist, who, in contrast to what Liu and Deng were doing, introduced various programmes to make the PLA a 'living school of Mao Zedong thought'.

A part of the story of Mao's counterattack is linked with the manner in which Mao managed to relate foreign policy and military affairs with internal politics. Mao's earlier dissatisfaction with the Soviet Union had many causes, but at the heart of the Sino–Soviet differences was the incompatibility between Khrushchev's view of 'peaceful coexistence' with the capitalist nations, headed by the USA, and Mao's insistence that Moscow support fraternal China's aggressive policies towards the West. The situation became particularly irksome when Moscow not only refused to back China's initiative against Taiwan in 1958 and against India in 1959, but showed its pique at Mao's attempts to disturb the international status quo by rescinding, in 1959, the Soviet agreement to supply China with a 'sample' nuclear bomb. This was taken as an insult by Mao, who in 1960, started to attack the Soviet leadership for 'revisionism', i.e., for revising egalitarian communist goals internally (by allowing the development of state capitalism and an elitist bureaucracy) and for surrendering to 'imperialist pressures' externally. As a result of this and other concerns, in 1960 the Soviets cut off their aid to China and withdrew their specialists; in the same year they signed a friendship treaty with India. In 1962, the year Moscow stood by India in her border war with China, the Sino–Soviet split was fully revealed, and for all practical purposes Sino–

Soviet relations ended for the next twenty years. From then till the early 1970s, China faced both the superpowers alone.

While these developments may have disturbed some of his comrades, Mao was not unhappy to have broken away from Moscow's yoke and, to have made China truly 'independent'. The Great Leader could now turn his attention fully to internal affairs where the party had allowed the re-emergence of the Soviet-style command system and, from Mao's point of view, prepared the conditions for the restoration of 'capitalism' and, thereby, for the rise of 'revisionism'. Mao could see the signs of this in the revival of private plots and free markets, the linking of market forces with the economy, and the emergence of privately-owned small enterprises.

The actions of the Pragmatists had been successful in reviving the economy shattered by the Leap, but in the process of putting the country back on the path of sound economic development, the Pragmatists had ignored Mao's repeated call that ideology and politics must remain in absolute command of all social, educational, and economic activities. They apparently had chosen to forget Mao's 1958 admonishment that 'those who pay no attention to politics and are busy with their work all day long will become economists who have gone astray and are dangerous'. They had also overlooked Mao's ominous warning, made in late 1959, that 'bourgeois elements have infiltrated the party'.

In 1962, when the memory of the 'three bitter years' had begun to fade, Mao became more forthright in airing his views. Knowing that he was not being listened to by party leaders, Mao repeated his 1957 tactic and spoke directly to 7,000 provincial and district party functionaries. It was evident that he was speaking out of frustration. There was danger, warned Mao, that China could become a 'bourgeois country' if it followed a revisionist line. He deplored the fact that some leaders were suppressing the revolutionary activity of the masses and were not allowing the masses to speak up, and he contemptuously denounced 'these comrades' for thinking that they were 'tigers and that nobody will dare touch their arse'. '*We must find a way to deal with this type of people*,' said Mao, '*and arrest some and execute a few*.' The Pragmatists still did not bother to take him seriously.

The Socialist Education Movement

Finally, in September 1962, at a plenary session of the Central Committee, the last formal party conference to be held till 1966, Mao made his stand more explicit and forced the party to launch a mass movement for ideological re-education aimed at raising the political consciousness of the cadres and masses to revive their flagging revolutionary spirit. Mao warned in his speech that throughout the historical period of socialism the bourgeoisie would continue to present a permanent threat of revisionism. The party had to remain vigilant and ceaselessly struggle against bourgeois thought. Therefore, class struggle could not, as yet, be ruled out. Mao also made a direct attack on the intellectuals who were using literature 'for anti-party activity' and creating a counterrevolutionary public opinion.

The new party rectification programme, which followed the Central Committee meeting, broadened into a nationwide Socialist Education Movement (SEM) which lasted from 1963 to 1965. Mao, himself, drafted the first set of 'ten points' that were supposed to provide the guidelines for the SEM. The campaign at this stage concentrated on the countryside and aimed at 'cleaning up' the 'unhealthy tendencies' that had arisen because of the post-GLF policies. The Pragmatists agreed with Mao that the work style of many of the basic level cadres had deteriorated and needed to be rectified. In the new bureaucratic command environment, many of these cadres had become corrupted and begun to take petty bribes and falsify accounts for personal gain. Naturally, this had alienated the peasantry and created a climate of distrust between the peasants and the party.

The Pragmatists, however, did not agree with Mao on the methods to be employed to carry out the 'clean up'. Mao wanted the party to go back to his 'mass-line' approach and mobilize the 'poor peasants and the lower middle peasants' for class struggle, get the peasants to criticize the cadres in mass meetings and pressure them to publicly confess their guilt. Only by following this course would the cadres be truly cleansed of their bourgeois thought and tendencies, and gain a proper socialist attitude. The programme would also help to elevate the political consciousness of the masses.

The Pragmatists, shuddering at the possibility of the country slipping into another GLF-type social upheaval, refused to accept Mao's thesis that a 'class struggle' was called for. Liu and Deng were convinced that the situation could be dealt with by disciplining and punishing the errant cadres without disturbing the social stability needed to ensure production targets. Therefore, they issued their own 'ten-points' (called the Later Ten Points to distinguish them from Mao's Former Ten Points). The Later Ten Points, drafted by Deng Xiaoping, the party secretary general, made rectification an internal party matter, and ordered urban-based work teams to visit the communes, investigate the work of the cadres and dole out punishment where needed.

After initial enquiries, when it was discovered that corruption was even more widespread than originally thought, Liu Shaoqi issued the Revised Later Ten Points in 1964, which made the party investigation of cadres more exhaustive. The thrust of the Pragmatists' approach, however, remained unchanged.

Mao could not accept this procedure because it implied a total rejection of his fundamental goals. The Pragmatists had managed to keep the peasant associations out of the picture and had refused to look upon the cadres' behaviour as being 'revisionist' and a class product. Punishment removed the erring cadres from their jobs but *did not* 'educate and transform' them. The party had substituted the right of the masses to supervise the cadres from below with administrative regulations from above.

Early in 1965, Mao for the last time tried to force the party to accept his political agenda by issuing a fresh set of directives for the SEM, the Twenty-Three Articles. This document went beyond the 'clean up' campaign in the countryside and declared that,

> The key point of the (SEM) is to *rectify those people in positions of authority within the party who take the capitalist road*, and to progressively consolidate and develop the socialist battlefront in the urban and the rural areas.
>
> Of those people in positions of authority who take the capitalist

> road, some are out in the open and some are concealed. Of the people who support them some . . . are at higher levels . . . .
>
> Among those at higher levels there are some people . . . even in the work of provincial and Central Committee departments, *who oppose socialism* . . . .
>
> Certain people do not distinguish the boundary between the enemy and ourselves; they have lost the class standpoint; and they harbour, within their own families and among their own friends and fellow workers, these people who engage in capitalist activities.

Although Mao's Twenty-Three Articles also failed to radicalize the Socialist Education Movement, they had prepared the groundwork for Mao's all-out attack on the Pragmatists, which followed in 1966.

The People's Liberation Army as a Model

While it was becoming abundantly clear that the party had failed to uphold Maoist values, the People's Liberation Army emerged as a model of Maoism. After taking over as minister of defence, Lin Biao had re-introduced political indoctrination programmes in the armed forces and heightened the role of the party within the army. Lin used Mao's writings to extol the simple revolutionary virtues of loyalty to the party and its great leader, hard work, disdain for material possessions, selflessness, altruism and so on. All the activities of the soldiers were related to ideology, and the thought of Mao Zedong was applied to the most mundane of circumstances; for example, one did not brush one's teeth to merely clean the teeth but because the act had an inner significance connected with Mao's call that the nation must acquire good habits of personal hygiene and cleanliness. By 1962, Lin had made the 'Thought of Mao Zedong' the basic fabric which held the PLA together.

In 1963, when civilian party cadres were being scrutinized for bad practices and the SEM was not being carried out in accordance with Mao's instructions, the army started a national 'learn from Lei Feng' campaign. Lei Feng, 'Chairman Mao's good soldier', was held up as a model for youth to follow. Lei Feng was an ordinary soldier who died at the age of twenty-two (in 1962) in a road accident, but in his brief life Lei had shown 'the most enduring, the most dogged, and the most praiseworthy revolutionary spirit in all aspects of routine work'. Lei worked exceedingly hard, always wondering how he could 'repay the party for its kindness'; he was 'full of gratitude for the new society' when he was given arduous tasks like tractor-driving or steel-making; Lei learnt to live simply, volunteer for jobs no one else wanted to do, suffer cold and hunger gladly, give away his property to those more needy than he, and spend his spare hours helping in commune work. He was always sacrificing himself for the greater cause and always studying Chairman Mao's instructions in order to better himself.

Lei left behind a diary which was published so that his 'shining example' could be followed by others.

In 1964, when his confrontation with the party was becoming more acute, Mao called upon the nation to 'Learn from the Experience of the PLA in Political Education and Ideological Work'. The article in the *People's Daily* which launched the campaign extolled the army men for their ardent love of the country, the people, socialism, and, more importantly, for being 'impartial and selfless. (Rendering) service to others without considering their own interests, they even sacrifice their valuable time and life for the sake of socialism'. In true Maoist fashion, military officers lived and worked with common soldiers for a certain period every year; in 1965 the officers gave up wearing special uniforms and insignia indicating rank.

The 'learn from the PLA' campaign was an obvious indication that Mao had lost faith in the party's ability to rectify itself and be a model of ideological purity, civic virtue and moral perfection. The campaign also provided Mao an opportunity to further strengthen the cult of personality. In 1964, the PLA published a pocket-size volume of *Quotations from Chairman Mao Zedong* with a distinguishing red jacket. The Little Red Book was distributed widely and in 1966, after Mao had toppled the Pragmatists, there was perhaps nobody in the country except pre-school children who did not carry it on his or her person.

EXCERPTS FROM LEI FENG'S DIARY

(1) Thinking of the past I feel an intense hatred for (imperialism, feudalism, and bureaucratic capitalism).

Thinking of the present I feel I owe unbounded gratitude to the Party and Chairman Mao for their kindness.

Looking at the future, I feel full of energy and confidence. I am determined to fight to the bitter end for the cause of communism.

(2) The people's great liberator, the great Chinese Communist Party, rescued me from a hell on earth . . . I feel in my bones that it is (the) happiest thing to live in a socialist society, in a big revolutionary family, in the great era of Mao Zedong . . . . Comparing the past with the present you feel an urge to think of everything in terms of revolution. We must hold high the red banner of Mao Zedong's thoughts and carry on the hard-working spirit and keep on other fine traditions of the revolutionary martyrs.

(3) Youth is beautiful. But real youth belongs to those who always aim high, work selflessly and are modest.

(4) To me Chairman Mao's works are like food, weapons and the steering wheel of a vehicle. To live you have food, to fight you must have a weapon, to drive a vehicle you must have a steering wheel, and to work for the revolution you must read Chairman Mao's works.

(5) November 8, 1960. I will never forget this day. This is the day when I had the honour of being made a member of the great Chinese Communist Party, thus realizing my highest goal.

Oh, how thrilled my heart is! It is beating with wild joy. How great the Party is! How great Chairman Mao is! Oh, Chairman Mao, it is you who have given me a new lease of life! When I was struggling in the fiery pit of hell and waiting for the dawn it was you who saved me, gave me food and clothing, and sent me to school! . . . It was under your constant care and guidance that I, a former poor orphan, became a Party member, a man with some knowledge and political consciousness.

Attack on Party Intellectuals

Parallel to the 'learn from the PLA' campaign, Mao started a movement to cleanse the literary and art circles of 'revisionism'. If the general body of the party needed 'socialist education', the intelligentsia needed a 'cultural revolution'. It is this campaign that finally provided the stratagem Mao was looking for to shatter the stronghold of the Pragmatists.

As noted earlier, party intellectuals such as Wu Han and Deng Tuo were becoming an anathema to the Maoists. Most of these writers were working under Peng Zhen, the politically powerful first secretary of the Beijing party committee and the mayor of Beijing, and were protected by him. In 1964, Mao, in a clever move, appointed Peng Zhen as the head of a committee to guide cultural reform; he would either have to take action against his protégés or be condemned for not doing so. Jiang Qing (Madame Mao Zedong), who had become an outspoken advocate of the Mao-ization of culture, was particularly anxious to replace traditional Beijing operas (which dealt with themes taken from imperial Chinese history) with revolutionary operas (based on stories from the Long March and so on). Peng Zhen, along with the other cultural bureaucrats, however, managed temporarily to deflect the thrust of the Maoist campaign.

Having failed to get the Beijing cultural establishment to take action, Mao moved the action to the more congenial environment of Shanghai and persuaded a minor party intellectual there (Yao Wenyuan) to publish a critique of *Hai Rui Dismissed from Office*, 'exposing Wu Han's anti-party and anti-socialist crimes'. Forced to take cognizance of this article, Peng Zhen still tried to blunt Mao's attack by allowing the *People's Daily* to publish the critique, but considering it as an 'academic' issue and not a political one. The Maoists responded by producing a document, approved by the Military Affairs Commission (of which Mao was chairman), that all academic questions must be judged in political terms, and Mao unleashed an attack on Peng Zhen for having obstructed the cultural revolution. Matters moved rather quickly thereafter. The Maoists took over the propaganda media and the Beijing municipal government; most of the leading figures in the cultural field, including Peng, were purged.

A new 'Cultural Revolution Group', manned by Maoists (including Jiang Qing), was established and it soon assumed extraordinary powers in the direction of the country's affairs.

The Great Proletarian Cultural Revolution Mao's Second Great Experiment With the Nation

On 16 May 1966, Mao issued a circular which became the programmatic document of the Great Proletarian Cultural Revolution (GPCR, or the Cultural Revolution for short). The document announced that the GPCR was an 'upsurge . . . pounding at all the decadent ideological and cultural positions still held by the bourgeoisie and the remnants of feudalism'. And it went on to declare that the GPCR must address itself to 'people of the Khrushchev brand (who) are still nestling in our midst', and the 'bunch of counterrevolutionary revisionists' who had 'sneaked into the party, the government and the army'. In a later article the Chinese people were told that the GPCR had to settle the basic question 'whether the proletariat or the bourgeoisie will win in the realm of ideology'.

After the failure of the Great Leap Forward, this was Mao's second attempt to impose his grand utopian vision on the Chinese nation. Having reached the age of seventy-three, Mao was in a hurry to achieve his goal before he died, and he did not hesitate to revert to unorthodox techniques to do so. The party had failed him by denying the role of class struggle and by replacing his style of revolutionary change with planned development. According to Mao, this had happened because, in the period of economic difficulties from 1959 to 1962, 'the demons and spirits came out of hiding' and the party and government came to be dominated by 'bourgeois revisionists'. It had, therefore, become absolutely necessary to purge the party of 'capitalist roaders' who had infiltrated leadership positions, cleanse and reorganize the party as a whole, and remove all persons in authority in the government bureaucracy, the educational and cultural fields, and the economic sector who had opposed the thought of Mao Zedong.

But all this was supposedly secondary to the main purpose of the GPCR: the spiritual transformation of the nation. Mao wanted to ensure that the youth could be depended upon to become the genuine revolutionary leaders of tomorrow when he was no longer there to guide them. Such an assurance could come only if the remnants of old thought, old culture, old customs, and old habits (the Four Olds) that tainted the people's minds, were replaced by proletarian revolutionary consciousness. Mao called for a revolution that would touch the very souls of the people.

At least in its early phase, the GPCR was guided from above, but in keeping with Mao's ideology that all revolutionary action must be based on a spontaneous mass movement, the Cultural Revolution soon came to be centred in a vast body of school and college students, the Red Guards of the revolution, who took the revolution into channels Mao could not have conceived of. Incited by Mao's call to rebel against reactionary power holders and fired by Mao's vision of the good society, the students responded with unbounded zeal and were soon active outside their campuses resolutely attacking 'all counterrevolutionary revisionists of the Khrushchev type and carry(ing) the socialist revolution through to the end'. Schools and colleges were closed for six months to allow the students to participate in the GPCR—they did not reopen till years later when Mao, himself, had to stop the tragic carnage and destruction he had let loose. During the summer and fall of 1966, ten to eleven million Red Guards came to Beijing to rally in front of Mao Zedong, the supreme commander of the Red Guards, in order to pledge their hearts to him. The following excerpt describes the rally on 18 August 1966:

> The rally began at 7.30 in the morning. As the band played *The East is Red*, Chairman Mao appeared on the Tiananmen tower . . . The crowds leapt with joy. A great many hands, holding red-covered *Quotations from Chairman Mao Zedong*, stretched towards the rostrum. A million warm hearts flew out to Chairman Mao and a million pairs of eyes sparkling with revolutionary fervour were turned on him. The crowd became even more excited when they noticed that their respected and beloved leader was wearing a plain cotton uniform. 'We feel Chairman Mao is closer to us in a military uniform,' they said. 'Chairman Mao always fights together with us.' Some remarked: 'We are wonderfully

happy to have such a supreme commander as Chairman Mao. We will always be his good fighters, follow him, and make revolution for the rest of our lives.'

The Cultural Revolution, unlike the Great Leap Forward, was primarily an urban phenomenon. It reflected Mao's deep-rooted suspicion of the urban intelligentsia, and as an extension thereof, his antagonism toward educational figures, writers and thinkers, technicians, economists, managers of industries and commerce, and bureaucrats—all representatives of the intelligentsia.

The Red Guards, armed with the Little Red Book and guided by the Great Leader's instructions such as 'destruction must precede construction', 'disorder was good', 'do not fear chaos', and 'learn revolution by making revolution', swept through the cities like a seething tidal wave destroying everything that came in their way. They occupied administrative offices in schools and colleges, tortured and humiliated the administrators and teachers and forced them to 'confess' their crimes against Chairman Mao. They denounced their own parents for harbouring old values; they entered any house they wanted and confiscated foreign-made articles, burnt all the books that appeared to have bourgeois content, and smashed antique art objects; they arrested persons 'contaminated' by Western culture (such as music composers or piano players); they cut off the hair of women sporting 'foreign' hairstyles; they changed the names of streets if they smacked of the past (for example 'Harmony Street' would be renamed 'Revolution Street'). Many citizens, like the famous writer Lao She, were beaten to death, while others were driven to suicide, and thousands were battered and maimed.

In the beginning, the Pragmatists tried to control the GPCR from above, just as they had done with the Socialist Education Movement, by sending 'work teams' to the schools and colleges and, in the words of the Maoists, 'using the Red Flag as a cover to attack the Red Flag'. They also tried to use Mao's dicta on the sanctity of the party to admonish the youth that it was 'not justified to rebel against the party'. Later, the Pragmatists tried to appease Mao by sacrificing a number of junior officials, but they had misread the situation. Mao was in no mood to get into any political chess games with them. By the end of 1966, Mao directed the several million strong army of the Red Guards to 'bombard the headquarters' and crush 'those in authority taking the capitalist road'.

Though no names were named, it was soon well understood that Mao was pointing to Liu Shaoqi and Deng Xiaoping. In mid-1967, after the Red Guards had mounted several massive demonstrations against Liu and Deng, Mao got an 'enlarged' Politburo Standing Committee (enlarged with pro-Maoists) to censure the two top leaders of China. Although they had confessed their 'mistakes', Liu was in jail by the end of the year, and Deng was exiled to the interior. Liu, chosen as his heir apparent by Mao himself, died in jail in 1969 after he had been officially denounced as a 'renegade, traitor and scab hiding in the party, a lackey of imperialism, modern revisionism and the Guomindang reactionaries'. Lin Biao, 'Mao Zedong's close comrade-in-arms', replaced Liu as Mao's designated successor.

The attack on Liu Shaoqi, the chairman of the People's Republic and the second most important man in the party, and the humiliating public trials of high-ranking party functionaries like Peng Zhen and Madame Liu Shaoqi, eroded the power of the Pragmatists, and in early 1967 the Red Guards, now joined by 'rebel' workers, took the call to 'seize power' seriously. Party bosses in the provinces, communes and factories were dragged out of their offices and paraded with dunce caps on their heads and signs round their necks indicating the nature of their crimes. How anarchic the situation had become by the summer of 1967 can be seen by the purges that had taken place at the very top of the party structure: seven members of the Politburo (out of thirteen), six members of the party Secretariat (out of ten), fourty-eight members of the Central Committee (out of ninety-three), and five regional party chiefs (out of six) had been purged. By the year's end the Politburo was non-existent, only thirty-six members of the Central Committee had survived, the six regional party bureaus were no longer functioning, and only five provincial party chairmen (out of twenty-eight) were still in office.

With the support of the PLA, the only institution that remained unimpaired, the collapsing party structure was replaced by Revolutionary Committees formed by 'three-way alliances' representing the revolutionary masses, the military and Maoist 'revolutionary' party cadres. The Revolutionary Committees became the new centres of power in the state and provincial organizations, propaganda media, schools and colleges, transportation and security departments, and industrial and other economic units.

The entry of the PLA as an active participant in the GPCR, and the establishment of the Revolutionary Committees in which the PLA played the dominant role, spelled the end of the monopoly of action enjoyed by the Red Guards. This was a strange twist to Mao's grand design to make the masses the true rulers of the country. Indeed, it was an indication that Mao had failed in his endeavour.

The roots of the failure lay in Mao's peculiar belief that somehow construction would follow destruction. While destruction had been relatively easy, construction needed a blueprint which was non-existent. Furthermore, the Red Guards were not a cohesive body of revolutionaries following any kind of common strategy. The Red Guards, themselves, were split into various factions, each considering itself more Maoist than the others; in Beijing alone there were three major factions of Red Guards struggling for power. In the provinces many local party leaders had anticipated developments by setting up their own Red Guard units who began to clash with pro-Mao Red Guards established by teams sent out by groups in Beijing. There was similar factionalism among the revolutionary worker groups. It is estimated that there were literally hundreds of self-styled Maoist groups in the country who kept the cities in constant turmoil by fighting each other.

The PLA could not be expected to remain a neutral witness to the disturbances created by the factional infighting of the revolutionaries. It began to side with the less radical groups and suppress the more violent ones in the interest of law and order. In April, the ultra-Maoists in the Cultural Revolution Group, led by Jiang Qing, had managed to influence Mao to counter this 'black current' by ordering the army not to use force against Maoist revolutionary organizations. Mao had got rid of all opposition within the party and government but was now caught between the need to save the country from civil war and the desire to carry on with the GPCR experiment. The moderate Zhou Enlai wanted Mao to tilt in favour of stability, but the exuberant Jiang Qing favoured a continuation of the GPCR.

The curbs placed on the army proved terribly costly. Thousands of so-called revolutionary factions, armed with all kinds of weapons, killed each other in pitched battles. The mood of the military can, perhaps, be judged from what happened in Wu Han. There armed clashes between two factions, the 'Proletarian Liaison Centre of Mao Zedong Thought Million Heroic Troops' and 'Mao Zedong Thought Fighting Team's Wuhan Workers' General Headquarters' which comprised a total membership of a million workers, had disrupted communications, halted production, brought life in the city to a standstill, and resulted in hundreds of deaths. The general in command of the Wu Han military region backed the more moderate Million Heroes against the Workers' Headquarters. The Cultural Revolution Group in Beijing did not approve and sent two emissaries to get the commander to change his stand. The military was so incensed that it helped the Million Heroes kidnap the emissaries and seize the city. This was 'mutiny', and though Beijing did not have to use force (gunboats and airborne troops had been rushed to the area) to suppress it, it could not ignore the possibility of more such occurrences. The incident, however, gave the ultra-Maoists a reason to purge the PLA of military officers considered anti-Maoists and to push the policy of 'arming the left'. This in turn encouraged the revolutionaries to raid army depots, where they acquired guns, heavy artillery and tanks. The country was brought to the verge of civil war.

No doubt realizing that a split in the army would mean the end of any sanity that was left in the country, Mao now veered back to Zhou Enlai's position and, in September 1967, not only ordered the revolutionaries to stop seizing military equipment from the PLA, but authorized the PLA to use force to deal with recalcitrant mass organizations.

The GPCR was finally in retreat. The military, helped by old party cadres who had organizational and bureaucratic experience, started the slow process of bringing back tranquility to a country which had seen so much turmoil, confusion and chaos. Students were asked to return to their schools, which were reopened in the fall of 1967 (though the universities remained closed till 1970), and workers were directed to turn their attention back to the business of production. But it was not that simple to bring back law and order by fiat, and the leftists' rear guard action and factional violence continued into the summer of 1968, when nearly 100,000 persons lost their lives in south China alone. A disillusioned Mao Zedong finally decided to turn his back on the Red Guards, his 'revolutionary successors', and on 28 July 1968, he summoned the quarrelling leaders of the students in Beijing to meet him. After reprimanding them for their lack of true revolutionary spirit he said, with tears in his eyes, 'You have let me down, and what is more, you have disappointed the workers, peasants, and soldiers of China.' Actually, Mao's rejection of the Red Guards had not come suddenly; as he had explained to a foreign delegation in August 1967:

> It was desired to bring up some successors among the intellectuals, but now it seems a hopeless task. As I see it, the intellectuals, *including young intellectuals still receiving education in school*, still have a basically bourgeois world outlook, whether they are in the party or out of it. This is because for 17 years after the liberation the cultural and educational circles have been dominated by revisionism. *As a result, bourgeois ideas are infused in the blood of the intellectuals.*

Mao's young intellectuals, who were supposed to imbibe the true Maoist virtues through the process of destroying the older intelligentsia, were found to be as tainted as their elders. They had proved themselves to be individualistic, selfish and corruptible. Peace was restored in the cities by transferring several million students, and twenty million other urbanites (mostly the unemployed), to the countryside for resettlement.

As the GPCR petered out, the Maoist revolutionaries were thrust aside, and the PLA took over the major role of re-establishing law and order, restrengthening administrative and control structures, and bringing back some sense of coherence to the nation.

An Evaluation of the GPCR

From virtually every point of view the Cultural Revolution proved to be a disastrous failure.

1. *Social Cost*: It has been estimated that nearly 500,000 persons lost their lives during the GPCR, and over 100,000,000 others suffered one way or the other from the activities of the 'revolutionary' student and worker groups. Since the Cultural Revolution was primarily an urban phenomenon, this means that fifty per cent of the urban population had come out of the experiment physically or psychologically damaged: millions had been tortured and beaten, dismissed from their jobs and sent to jails and labour camps; millions lost one or more members of their families; millions had their property confiscated or destroyed. Practically all of the affected people had been subjected to kangaroo courts and public humiliation.

Though primary and middle schools remained closed for only two years, the suspension of enrollment into all universities for six years (post-graduate admissions were suspended for twelve years) left a gap in higher education which is currently proving to be a handicap in China's modernization programmes.

On the larger plane, the rabid anti-intellectual bias of Mao Zedong encouraged the most ferocious attacks on the intelligentsia. University professors, schoolteachers, scientists, technologists, writers, artists, journalists, musicians, and professionals in every field were 'overthrown', persecuted and humiliated. A good number were sent down to the villages for 'thought reform through labour'. The frenzied Red Guards beat several to death and hounded several others to commit suicide. Even after they had been rehabilitated a few years later, the intellectuals were reluctant to take up their old activities of research and writing lest they be condemned for being 'specialists'. There was a drastic reduction in the number of books published (with the exception of the Little Red Book) during the GPCR, and of the 790 periodicals published in 1966 only 22 survived in 1968. The country had become culturally barren.

Lastly, by encouraging the youth to denounce their parents and elders and look with scorn upon traditional patterns of courteous behaviour, the GPCR vulgarized and brutalized society. After Mao's death, party leaders had to launch various campaigns to extol the virtues of politeness and proper decorum and try to get the youth of China to be less rude in their language and deportment.

(2) *Ideology and the Party*: Mao had launched the GPCR to perpetuate his notion of 'ceaseless revolution'. In Mao's view, since the party was moving towards institutionalized government and establishing bureaucratic structures that had no place for mass campaigns and revolutionary fervour, he had to weaken the control of the party over the country. He was successful in doing so, but with what result? Mao may have believed that China was a 'blank sheet of paper' and that, once the Pragmatists were overthrown, he would have absolute power to indoctrinate the nation. In fact, however, Mao found that he had to work under several constraints, the primary one being that he could not allow the Cultural Revolution to wholly demolish the existing institutions of party and government. As the man at the helm, Mao himself had to ensure the continuity of the state and of economic production by guaranteeing a modicum of national stability. Therefore, he had to limit the extent of chaos generated by the revolutionaries.

Moreover, Mao needed a cadre of absolutely trustworthy and highly experienced Maoist ideologues who could be used for both the negative and positive goals of the Cultural Revolution: as a weapon to attack the existing institutions and as an instrument for the re-education of the people and the reorganization of the national structures. The Red Guards proved to be totally incapable of such a monumental task.

As a consequence, Mao could neither fulfil his goal of liquidating his 'revisionist' enemies nor of re-educating the nation. On the contrary, he was forced to give up 'mass action' and allow the PLA and the moderate party leaders (headed by Zhou Enlai) to intervene in the GPCR. The intrusion of the PLA into civil politics was, however, a matter of considerable worry to Mao, who had always insisted that the 'gun will be in the hands of the party, and not the other way around'. Therefore, soon after the Red Guards had been disbanded and the Cultural Revolution technically, though not officially, brought to a halt, Mao had to accept Zhou Enlai's policy of rehabilitating erstwhile 'rightist' party leaders, including the 'number two capitalist roader' Deng Xiaoping, because their experience was needed to reconstruct the shattered party and state structures.

The major reason for Mao's failure was located in Mao's ideology itself, because the ideology was neither well-defined nor did it present a cohesive body of ideas. For example, Mao's insistence that China carry on 'class warfare', not on the basis of class origin but on the basis of 'class consciousness', was an ambiguous and potentially dangerous idea. Who was to say what 'bourgeois consciousness' meant? Anybody could be accused of being tainted by 'bourgeois thought' and attacked as an enemy of the masses, as often happened during the GPCR. Innumerable examples exist of Red Guards beating up persons wearing pointed shoes, or trousers tailored in Hong Kong, or having a bowl of gold fish in their homes, because these actions connoted bourgeois tendencies. Similarly, Mao's ideas of 'mass line' could never be adequately defined or institutionalized. (In any case, how could the Red Guards be considered 'the masses'?) Finally, Mao's ideology, which ostensibly was intended to liberate the masses (we presume the word means 'the common people') from unthinking obedience to bureaucratic authority, had the contrary effect of forcing them to offer unquestioning obedience to him. As Lin Biao remarked in Mao's presence, 'We must carry out Mao Zedong's ideas when we understand them and even when we do not understand them.'

The GPCR did irreparable damage to the CCP. Mao had sullied the image and prestige of the party by attacking the most venerable and nationally-honoured leaders of the party. Furthermore, as the GPCR proceeded, even the accepted 'leftist' of today became the 'rightist' of tomorrow, and several members of the very Maoist Cultural Revolution Group were successively purged. Nobody was sure anymore as to what constituted the correct policy, and what the incorrect. During the GPCR the party was no longer the source of legitimacy; all legitimacy came from an adherence to the Thought of Mao Zedong. In practice this meant that legitimacy came from the faction that was the nearest to The Supreme Leader and had his blessing. After Mao's death, when Mao and Maoism came under attack, the latter source of legitimacy also disappeared. The unchallenged authority that the CCP had enjoyed when it first came to power was undermined, and it has yet to recover its original eminence and popularity. A great part of the confusion that has marked the current crisis of authority in China can be traced to this development.

(3) *Foreign Relations*: Though our story of communist China con-

centrates on inner developments, it is pertinent to mention briefly the impact of the GPCR on China's international relations. After the break with the Soviet Union, China had adopted a policy which encouraged revolutionary movements in the countries of the Third World and tried to wean them away from the superpowers. This policy met with serious setbacks by 1965, but just as China was in the process of being further isolated, the GPCR was launched and Mao voluntarily withdrew China from the larger world order so that the country's entire attention could be turned inward. All Chinese students studying abroad, and all Chinese ambassadors, except for the one in Egypt, were recalled.

The animus of the Cultural Revolution against things foreign and the mass-movement style of politics had their impact on the work of the ministry of external affairs, which was physically occupied by the Red Guards in 1967. Foreign Minister Chen Yi was humiliated and obliged to make self-criticism. Under the circumstances, the government could not stop the Red Guards from harassing foreign diplomats residing in Beijing, particularly the 'revisionist' Russians and the 'imperialist' British. Because of the British actions in Hong Kong to contain revolutionary activity in the colony, the British embassy in Beijing was burned and the British diplomatic staff, including Charge d'Affaires Sir Donald Hopson and the women employees, severely manhandled and beaten. Hopson was left 'more or less unconscious and bleeding like a pig'.

After the Cultural Revolution was brought to a halt and Zhou Enlai regained control over the ministries of government, foreign policy once again became more conventional and pragmatic.

Mao's Last Years, 1969–76

The violent stage of the GPCR ended in 1969, but factional conflict and the 'struggle between the two lines' continued till Mao's death. The post-Mao leaders, therefore, refer to the entire period from 1966 to 1976 as the 'ten bad years' of the Cultural Revolution.

One major element that influenced the politics of this decade was China's changed perception of the world balance of power. In 1968, the Soviet Union intervened militarily in the internal affairs of Czechoslovakia to prevent the subversion of communism in that country. Based on the Brezhnev Doctrine that Moscow had the right to protect 'socialism' in any country of the socialist commonwealth, the action had an ominous ring for many Chinese leaders. Was Moscow reinforcing its military in northeast Asia as a prelude to similar action in China after Mao's death? Beijing condemned the Soviet invasion of Czechoslovakia in the strongest terms possible. At the same time, China viewed with alarm American intentions to pull out of Vietnam and reduce the US military presence in Asia as whole, because that would tilt the balance of global power in favour of Moscow.

A Chinese ambush of Soviet troops on an island in the Ussuri River in 1969 brought matters to a head. This ill-considered action may have been taken by the ultra-Maoists who hated to see the country give up its righteous revolutionary international stand, but the manner in which the Soviets trounced the Chinese had the opposite effect: Mao shifted his support away from Lin Biao and accepted Zhou Enlai's moderate internal and external policies. Secret negotiations were opened with the United States, leading to Nixon's dramatic visit to Beijing in February 1972 and the subsequent opening of relations between the two countries.

Internal Politics

During the last seven years of his rule, during most of which time he was seriously ill, Mao used his personal power to try to save as many of his revolutionary goals as he could. This was a futile effort in the long run because Mao could not work through any dependable, stable institution, since none existed. All he could do was to use his exalted personal status to manipulate affairs by shifting his support, back and forth, between two quarrelling factions: the Leftists (led by Madame Mao) and the Moderates (led by Zhou Enlai). That Mao could not even trust the Jiang Qing group to represent his ideology indicates how he had totally failed to institutionalize his values.

The third faction, the PLA, having acquired an increasingly prominent role in the government and the party through its place in the Revolutionary Committees and because Marshal Lin Biao had been designated Mao's successor, lost out in the power struggle when Mao became suspicious of Lin's ambitions and turned against him in 1970. In 1971, Lin Biao allegedly decided not to wait for Mao's death to gain power, but to acquire it immediately by carrying out a *coup d'etat*. According to the official version of the affair, Lin failed in his attempt to assassinate Mao and fled the country in a plane, heading for the Soviet Union. The plane crashed in Outer Mongolia, killing Lin and the other conspirators who had accompanied him. Lin's death, and the purge of pro-Lin elements in the PLA that followed, reduced the prestige of the PLA and gave Zhou an opportunity to further strengthen the party with rehabilitated old-timers. That the GPCR and the much-touted mass-line had done little to increase democracy in China was evidenced by the fact that Lin's death remained unreported in China for a whole year!

Jiang Qing and her three loyal lieutenants (the 'Gang of Four'), in anticipation of Mao's death, tried to build up their power by posing as true Maoists and by continuing to push for the GPCR policies in the fields of education, culture, and economy. But the suave and wily Zhou Enlai, the man who had held the post of premier from the day the PRC was established and who had managed to survive the upheavals of the GLF and the GPCR, somehow always succeeded in deflecting the attacks of the Gang of Four. He even persuaded a reluctant Mao to go along with policies that partially reversed the GPCR goals and permitted Zhou to rehabilitate many of the dismissed party leaders and even revive 'evil' economic practices related to material incentives.

The most important person to emerge from forced retirement was Deng Xiaoping, the former secretary-general of the party, who was appointed a vice-premier by Zhou Enlai in 1973; he was elected to the Politburo a year later. In early 1975, when it was apparent to the ailing Zhou that he did not have long to live, he elevated Deng to the post of First vice-premier (heading the list of twelve vice-premiers); Deng was also made a member of the standing committee of the Politburo, vice-chairman of the party, vice-chairman of the party's Military Commission, and appointed chief-of-staff of the PLA. Obviously, Deng was being groomed to take over as premier after Zhou died.

When the fourth National People's Congress (the Chinese parliament) was convened in Beijing in January 1975 (the third NPC was held in 1964) Zhou left his hospital sickbed to present his state of the nation address. The Congress was dominated by Zhou's faction of the party and government veterans and, perhaps for this reason, was not attended by Mao Zedong. Zhou emphasized the need for 'revolutionary unity' so that China could concentrate on the task of economic development, and his speech made the first reference to 'the Four Modernizations', which were to become the focus of developmental policies in post-Mao China:

> The first stage is to build an independent and relatively comprehensive industrial and economic system . . . before 1980; the second stage is to accomplish the *comprehensive modernization of agriculture, industry, national defence and science and technology* before the end of the century so that our national economy will be advancing in the front ranks of the world.

Zhou also very cleverly used one of Mao's statements that China should 'rely mainly on our own efforts while making external assistance subsidiary' in order to modify Mao's stand on 'self-reliance' and open China to the importation of Western technology. After the congress closed, Zhou returned to the hospital and for all practical purposes handed over the day-to-day work of the party and state to Deng. And Deng, with far less circumspection than Zhou, began to undo the practice of the Cultural Revolution that had weakened the educational, cultural and economic life of the nation. He also began to advocate policies of broader economic relations with the more developed states of the world.

The restoration of pragmatic policies disturbed the Maoists, and Mao showed his displeasure by commenting in his New Year's message of 1976 that 'stability and unity do not mean writing off class struggle; class struggle is the key link and everything else hinges on it'.

Zhou Enlai passed away on 8 January 1976. It is a sad commentary on the nature of Chinese politics that Mao did not think it fitting to attend the memorial service for one of the nation's most gifted and outstanding personalities, a man who had contributed so much to the building of new China. If this was because Mao was ailing, he could at least have paid a public tribute, which he did not do. On the contrary, the Party Centre.

reflecting Mao's inclination, issued an order that forbade all further expression of public grief after the memorial service was over. The intensity of Mao's disapproval of what Zhou had stood for was revealed on 7 February, when Mao appointed a relatively unknown party figure, Hua Guofeng, as acting premier, instead of giving that office to the more qualified Deng Xiaoping.

With Zhou out of the way, the Jiang Qing faction, with Mao's backing, began a campaign of vilification against Deng, accusing him of still harbouring 'bourgeois ideology'. Articles condemning Deng in the GPCR-style as the 'party person in power taking the capitalist road' and the 'capitalist roader trying to reverse verdicts' began to appear in increasing numbers. Finally, Mao endorsed the campaign with the petulant comment that, 'This person does not grasp class struggle . . . . He still continues his theme of "white cat, black cat", making no distinction between imperialism and capitalism.' This encouraged the leftists to even denigrate the memory of Zhou Enlai and assail his four modernizations programme as being 'revisionist'.

The struggle for power had come out into the open, and the citizens of Beijing, a million of whom had stood in the bitter January cold to watch Zhou's hearse pass by, were enraged by the insensitivity of the Maoist leaders. The traditional Qing Ming festival, when the Chinese honour their dead ancestors by sweeping their graves and putting flowers on them, fell on 4 April, and the citizens of Beijing seized this opportunity to pay their respects to Zhou Enlai. Beijingers, who had resented the order of the Maoists that they remove their black arm-bands, now began to demonstrate their love and admiration for Zhou by placing wreaths in his memory at the foot of the Monument to the People's Heroes in Tiananmen Square. The first wreath appeared on 19 March.

The Tiananmen Incident, 1976: A Citizen's Rebellion

Hua Guofeng, pressured by the leftists, declared the Qing Ming festival to be an outmoded, feudal, reactionary 'festival of ghosts', and forbade the citizens from taking part in it. But to no avail. By 4 April, two million citizens as individuals or as groups representing factories, government offices, military units, schools, and communes had visited the Square, and the pile of wreaths, bouquets of flowers, eulogies attached to Zhou's portraits, poems and posters rose to a height of fifty feet. It is possible that Deng had some hand in all this, but by all accounts it was a genuine outpouring of popular sentiment.

That the much-maligned intellectuals, whom the Maoists had dubbed the 'stinking ninth category' (following the eight other categories of reactionaries and counterrevolutionaries), played an important part in the Tiananmen Incident is indicated by the hundreds of poems and tracts, written in highly polished Chinese, that were left at the monument. Many of them, like the poem quoted below, were poignant expressions of protest:

> Devils howl as we pour out our grief,
> We weep but the wolves laugh,
> We shed our blood in memory of the hero,
> Raising our heads, we unsheathe our swords.

Under orders from the Maoist leaders, the police removed the wreaths and tore down the poems and placards in the early hours of the morning of the 5th while Beijing still slept. The authorities issued no communique and offered no explanation. The moment the citizens learned what had happened they rushed to Tiananmen Square shouting slogans and demanding that their wreaths be returned to them. A police loudspeaker van that tried to get them to disperse by announcing that they were being led astray by 'a handful of class enemies' was overturned by the angry crowd. The crowd, disregarding all official orders, continued to grow in size, and later more security vehicles were damaged or burned.

At 9.35 p.m, on the evening of 5 April, the lights of the Square were suddenly turned on, and a huge force of police and militia armed with clubs encircled the unarmed demonstrators and began a bloody and a ruthless assault. Estimates of the number of people killed and injured vary, but it can be safely assumed that hundreds died and many more hundred were brutally battered; several thousand were arrested. Even after it had been scrubbed away, the blood on the paving stones of Tiananmen Square left brown patches that reportedly were visible for months afterwards.

The Gang of Four denounced the demonstrators as 'counterrevolutionary' and blamed Deng for instigating the incident. They managed to get Deng dismissed from all posts inside and outside the party (7 April), but had to accept Mao's choice of Hua Guofeng as premier and first vice-chairman of the party. On 30 April, Mao legitimized Hua's succession by sending him a hand-written note that said: 'With you in charge, I am at ease.'

Four months later, on 9 September 1976, Mao Zedong passed away at the age of eighty-two. The radicals made a bid for power and tried to get Jiang Qing appointed chairman of the party. (It was later revealed that the Gang of Four not only had no power base, they were immensely disliked and feared by most segments of the party, the government and the military, if not by the entire nation.) However, the possibility of a political crisis was avoided when Hua, backed by the military–bureaucratic complex and senior party leaders,took pre-emptive action and arrested the Gang of Four on 6 October 1976. The country heaved a sigh of relief. The Maoist era had ended.

4

China After Mao
Deng Xiaoping's 'Second Revolution'

Deng Xiaoping probably had grand plans to celebrate the fortieth anniversary of the founding of the People's Republic on 1 October 1989; it would also have been an occasion to mark the successful conclusion of a decade of reforms carried out under his guidance. Unfortunately, the Tiananmen Massacre cast a pall over the country and focussed national attention on the economic imbalances and social disparities created by the reforms. The popular verdict was that economic growth, however striking, was not necessarily acceptable if it was uneven and not accompanied by equally far-reaching political reforms. The Reformers, consequently, have been forced to make a sober re-examination of their policies and their priorities.

China in the '80s and '90s

In the fourteen years following Mao's death, China has undergone a radical transformation so extensive in scale and so diversified in content that scholars have yet to comprehend it in all its implications. For a foreigner who had witnessed life in Mao's China and who revisited the country recently, say, in 1988, the visible changes alone would have been mind-boggling.

Though the crush of population in thc cities has increased, the depressing uniformity of the ubiquitous blue Mao jackets and blue trousers that were compulsory wear for both men and women in the old days has disappeared and given way to a pleasing variety of fashionable Western-style clothing. The visitor would have been struck by the vitality of city life: high-rise buildings, shops packed with consumer goods, eye-catching billboards and placards advertising a wide assortment of items ranging from cars, television sets, refrigerators, washing machines, watches, cameras, audio systems, clothing and swimming suits to cosmetics—items which few would have dreamed of possessing before 1976. Though the number of Chinese owning private cars is still small, the very fact that they now can do so is symbolic of the profundity of the shift from Mao's egalitarian policies; many of the other consumer commodities have reached even the homes of peasants.

Similar changes have enriched China's cultural life. Publishing houses are booming, and our visitor would have seen book stores crowded with people anxious to acquire the latest literature as it came off the press—new books are often sold out within days. He would also have noted that the Chinese could buy foreign magazines and books, see foreign operas, plays, and movies, attend foreign musical performances, and go to exhibitions of modern art (Chinese and foreign). Life generally had become more lively and vibrant.

Since one goal of the post-Mao Open Door policy was to attract tourist dollars, it is understandable why massive efforts have been made to make the foreigner comfortable. Every city in China now has a number of modern, multi-storeyed, centrally airconditioned hotels (often built with foreign collaboration), where one can order most foreign alcoholic beverages, eat in specialized restaurants that serve French, Italian, and other European foods, work out in a health club, and indulge in disco dancing. The tourist can also order a limousine to go and play golf in an elaborate, international-standard gold course, or visit a fashion show and buy designer clothes with Gucci or Pierre Cardin labels. Special shops and outlets dealing with Chinese antiques, handicrafts, silks, and so on, meant only for foreigners (the shops do not accept Chinese currency), are enticingly spread across the cities and outlying tourist spots. Over a million foreign tourists (not counting overseas Chinese) visited China and patronized this segment of the Chinese economy in the year prior to the Tiananmen Massacre.

The primary objective of the Open Door policy is, of course, to revitalize Chinese economic growth by importing foreign technology, scientific know-how, and investment. As a consequence, particularly in Beijing and Shanghai, but also in other major cities, there is a new cosmopolitan ambience, with a large number of signboards in every major foreign language that provide eloquent testimony to the vast array of foreign business houses, banks, and airlines that have rushed into China to profit from the new openness. The presence of American, British, German, Japanese, French, and other businessmen, technical specialists, lawyers, journalists, and thousands of foreign teachers and students, adds a unique 'foreign' flavour to the social environment of the Chinese cities.

Although Japan emerged as China's biggest trading partner (after Hong Kong), the Chinese considered America to be the country most vital to their development of science and technology. Our visitor would have been struck by the craze for things American, from spoken and written American-English to blue jeans and disco dancing. He would have got the impression that every Chinese had come to believe that he or she would somehow personally benefit from learning the English language, which was not only being taught in schools and colleges, but through lessons broadcast by the television and radio networks; thousands listened to Voice of America programmes to improve their spoken English. The visitor would have found himself frequently surrounded by Chinese people, from all walks of life, who would have tried to strike up a conversation in an effort to practice their English.

We have advisedly used the past tense in parts of the above section because, although much of what has been described remains true even today, some things have changed after the Tiananmen Massacre. Most notably, the tensions in Sino-Western relations have undermined the old openness, and a visitor today will find the Chinese reluctant to talk to him; indeed, they consciously avoid making any contact with foreigners. Since the government has suggested that there was a 'foreign hand' in the student movement, and has pointedly attacked the Voice of America for having played a nefarious role in the Tiananmen 'rebellion', no Chinese can now dare to be seen listening to VOA programmes or reading American magazines.

The visible changes described above, however extensive they may be, are only a reflection of the many fundamental reforms that have been introduced in post-Mao China to restructure the Chinese economy and the working of the Chinese government. These reforms are fittingly associated with the name of Deng Xiaoping, who has come to assume a Mao-like national leadership role and who has been accepted as the new Supreme Leader.

Deng came to power in 1978 by skilfully outmanoeuvering the inexperienced Hua Guofeng and getting him to resign his posts of party chairman and prime minister; Deng replaced Hua with his own protégés. Since then Deng has led a movement to undo Maoist policies and practices. Deng has made economic modernization his key goal and supplanted Mao's 'politics in command', 'mass-line' and 'mass mobilization' approaches with policies that are aimed at bringing stability to the state and ensuring steady economic development.

To fulfil this task, Deng has had to spread his efforts in many directions. Briefly, Deng has abolished party offices that allowed one leader to assume overwhelming authority and has introduced regulations that aim to reduce, ultimately to eliminate, the party's power to interfere in the administration of the country. In the course of time, if Deng's plans (which have suffered a setback after the Tiananmen Massacre) work out, party leadership should become more collective, and the functions of the party, the government, and the PLA (functions that had become confused with the establishment of the Revolutionary Committees) would be separated.

Deng has also forced veteran leaders to retire (till recently only death could remove a cadre from office) and give way to more educated and professional younger cadres by instituting rules and regulations governing tenure in office. Deng has advanced the cause of economic modernization (the main focus of his 'revolution') tremendously by rehabilitating the intellectuals, giving them an honoured place in society, and providing them a more liberal environment to function in. In the same strain, Deng has made 'expertness' more important than 'redness' and revamped the educational system.

To make the new system secure, Deng has established legal codes (law had a stunted development under Mao) that, one hopes, will protect the rights of the citizenry.

Lastly, Deng has encouraged the replacement of ideological incentives with material incentives, sanctioned an important role for private and collective enterprise, and is working towards the goal of replacing the old command economy with a free market. These policies are intended to release the productive capacity of the country and bring efficiency and rationalism to its economy.

Although Deng does not share Mao's major goals, there are many interesting parallels between the two great leaders. Like Mao, Deng is driven by a consuming passion to fulfil his vision before he dies and to restructure the party and state in such a fashion that his programmes will continue even after his death. In some ways, Deng so far has been more successful than Mao; whereas Mao failed to create the 'socialist society' he wanted to, Deng has been successful in changing the economic face of China.

However, like Mao, Deng has found it impossible to acquire absolute power and has had to work with factions within the party that oppose his economic policies because they are taking China away from the path of socialism. Like Mao, Deng has tried, and failed, to designate dependable successors who could be trusted to carry on his policies after he passes from the scene. Mao successively appointed Liu Shaoqi and Lin Biao as his chosen successors and then had to get rid of them; similarly, Deng appointed Hu Yaobang, only to later replace him with Zhao Ziyang. But then in 1989 he dismissed Zhao from all the posts he was holding. Mao eventually left the succession to a most unlikely candidate, Hua Guofeng, who was easily displaced by Deng. Deng, eighty-six years old in 1990, has now chosen Jiang Zemin, whose last important job was first secretary of the party in Shanghai. It is questionable whether Jiang has the requisite political backing of all the stronger factions and that he will be able to hold on to his high position after Deng dies.

Finally, like Mao, Deng has not been able to win over the intelligentsia and contain 'dissidence', in spite of all his efforts. After the Tiananmen Massacre, Deng, like Mao, has had to condemn the scholars and intellectuals who participated in the 'democracy movement' as 'counter-revolutionaries', using the old Maoist formula of 'class struggle' to eliminate them.

The student demonstrations actually reflected a deeper problem: Deng's reforms, however successful in the economic field, had failed to produce a more just and equitable society. Indeed, many of the social and political problems that had surfaced were a by-product of China's economic success.

These issues will be discussed in greater detail later in the chapter, but suffice it to say here that the personalized nature of Chinese politics has made Deng indispensable to the party. In Mao style, Deng remains at the helm of affairs although he has reached the venerable age of eighty-six.

Deng's ruthless suppression of the student-led 'democracy movement', and his subsequent re-emphasis of the dictatorial role of the party and his re-iteration that national life should be guided by some of the classical Maoist virtues (such as dedication to ideology and self-sacrifice), appear to have turned the clock back on his own modernization programme.

Deng Xiaoping's Return to Power and the Democracy Movement

Mao's death had created a potentially dangerous political vacuum. However, Hua Guofeng's arrest of the Gang of Four allayed the immediate fears of most of the leaders because it removed the threat of an ultra-left takeover. And since everyone was anxious that the succession question be handled peacefully, Hua Guofeng, already the prime minister, was hastily made chairman of the party and of the Military Affairs Commission, posts previously held by Mao. On the surface Hua was now the most powerful leader in the country, combining in his person the erstwhile authority of both Mao Zedong and Zhou Enlai. In reality, since Hua had no constituency of his own except the centre-leftists, who were not very powerful, he had to depend heavily on the backing of the Pragmatists in the party: the bureaucracy and the PLA (the supporters of Zhou Enlai and Deng Xiaoping). The price he had to pay for this support was the rehabilitation of Deng Xiaoping in 1977, and that concession ultimately became the cause of Hua's downfall.

Hua Guofeng tried to gain legitimacy by stressing his loyalty to Mao Zedong and Mao's ideology and by insisting that whatever policies chairman Mao had enunciated, and whatever instructions he had left behind (later referred to as the 'two whatevers'), must be strictly upheld and unquestioningly adhered to. Since Mao's note to Hua, 'with you in charge, I am at ease', could be construed as an instruction to the nation to accept Hua as its leader, the one to whom Mao had passed the sceptre, the 'two whatevers' policy had a natural appeal for Hua and his small clique. A glaring flaw in this strategy was that Hua could not explain why Deng, who had been criticized and dismissed by Mao, had been rehabilitated.

As more and more veteran comrades, who had been expelled during the Cultural Revolution, came to be rehabilitated, Mao's policies of that period also came under scrutiny. Even the arrest of the very Maoist Gang of Four had a negative repercussion for Hua because it opened the 1976 'Tiananmen Incident' for re-examination. Did he agree with the verdict that the people's 'sympathy demonstration' for Zhou Enlai had been counterrevolutionary? If he did not, and obviously he could not, then how could he explain the role he had played in condemning the good citizens of Beijing and in the dismissal of Deng? Hua was cornered.

In contrast to Hua, Deng (whose rehabilitation had given him back his old posts, including that of vice-premier) not only had the backing of most of the senior party and military figures, but had gained broader support from the people as a whole because of his declaration that he intented to make a break with China's recent past.

Deng countered Hua's 'two whatevers' with his own Maoist guideline, 'Seek truth from facts' (a statement Mao had made in his earlier years). Both sides used the press to publicize their stands; the aim was not just to convert the readers to either point of view, but to get the majority of the factions to accept one side and reject the other. By the fall of 1978, Deng had emerged as the victor in this inner-party struggle and his policies were confirmed at the historic Third Plenum of the Eleventh Central Committee meeting in December. The communique issued at the end of the session declared that the Gang of Four (read Mao) had:

> Arbitrarily described the political line and the achievements of (Deng in) 1975 as a 'right-deviationist wind to reverse correct verdicts'. This reversal of history must be reversed again. The session points out that the Tiananmen events of 5 April 1976 were entirely revolutionary actions . . . . The plenary session decided to *cancel the erroneous documents issued by the Central Committee in regard to (Deng Xiaoping) and the Tiananmen events.*

The meeting also rehabilitated Peng Dehuai (posthumously), Peng Zhen, and all other comrades (surely this could only mean a condemnation of Mao since the Gang of Four was not even there when Peng was ousted) except Liu Shaoqi, whose name and honour finally were redeemed in 1981; it rejected Hua's 'two whatevers' policy and 'pointed out that historical questions must be settled with the principle consistently advocated by Comrade Mao Zedong, that is, seeking truth from facts and *correcting mistakes whenever discovered*'. The session promised to look into the mistakes and shortcomings of the Cultural Revolution in due course 'so as to unify the views of the whole party and the people of the whole country'.

'Democracy and Human Rights' Movement, 1979

The outcome of the contest between Hua and Deng should never have been in doubt. Hua, in comparison to Deng, was a novice in the complex art of Chinese politics. Deng had been a party member for over half-a-century (Hua was just learning how to walk when Deng joined the party) and a member of the Politburo for a quarter-century (against Hua's four years in 1977), and Deng had a popular standing in the party and the army. However, in his campaign to undermine Hua, Deng also used a new weapon: a vocally supportive public opinion. Here he was helped by the fact that millions of people who had been victimized during the 'ten bad years' of the Cultural Revolution were as anxious as Deng to get 'unjust verdicts reversed'.

Late in 1978, encouraged by the Pragmatists, Beijingers whose suffering during the Cultural Revolution had been particularly intense and who had been further alienated when their pro-Zhou Enlai demonstrations in

1976 had been denounced as counterrevolutionary, began to put up posters on the so-called Democracy Wall (which stood in Beijing's western district) expressing their frustrations, grievances and opinions. The writers of the posters described the humiliations and tortures they had endured; they voiced their bitterness against the cadres who had refused interviews and turned down their applications for housing or jobs; they condemned the Gang of Four for having struck down Deng Xiaoping; some of them went so far as to censure Mao for having 'become metaphysical in his old age' and letting all these heinous crimes take place; and they voiced the hope that China would develop more democracy in the new era. These were heady days, and it appeared that free speech had finally come to China.

Poster after poster in Beijing took up the theme of 'feudal fascist despots' who had 'suppressed the revolutionary masses' and lamented that these despots could not be brought to justice because they were 'still holding power'. Soon similar posters began to appear in other major cities of China. This poster campaign contributed to the building up of an environment in which popular opinion was becoming increasingly anti-Hua and strongly pro-Deng. The Hua clique tried to put constraints on the movement, but the Pragmatists would not let that happen. Deng himself commented in November 1978 that:

> This is a normal phenomenon, a manifestation of the stable situation in our country .... We have no right to negate or criticize the masses for promoting democracy and putting up posters. The masses should be allowed to vent their grievances.

However, once the Third Plenum of the Eleventh Central Committee had met in December 1978 and Hua had been removed from centre stage, Deng began to have second thoughts about the 'democracy movement'. The reason is not far to seek. The protesters had gone beyond acceptable limits by enlarging the field of their criticism to include socialism itself and by demanding all kinds of human and democratic rights, not excluding Western-style democracy. To air their 'heretical' views they also established clubs, such as the Enlightenment Society and the China Human Rights Alliance, and began to publish journals, such as *Enlightenment*,

Democratic Forum and *Beijing Spring*. The ideas expressed by the young intellectuals came primarily from their negative personal experience that had led them to make a critical enquiry of the harsh political system in which they lived. Their conclusions were no doubt strengthened and even perhaps influenced by foreign writings that were now more readily available than ever before, which they could read in the original language or in translation. The new openness was also helpful in another way: it made it possible for them to meet and discuss their ideas with foreign journalists, diplomats, teachers, and other visitors who were equally keen to make friends with the Chinese intellectuals.

The national trend towards more openness to the outside world reached euphoric heights in early 1979 when Sino-American relations were normalized (1 January). Deng Xiaoping made a triumphant tour of the United States in February, and the first group of Chinese students arrived in America the same month to begin extended studies in US universities. Told that they must strive to catch up with the West, Chinese intellectuals and urbanites, who had been isolated for years from outside contact, welcomed everything foreign with unabashed eagerness. Deng may have wanted them to restrict their enthusiasm to foreign technology and science, but he could not contain the America mania that ensued.

The most troublesome aspect of the hurried way in which the Chinese were absorbing things American (from Deng's point of view) was not the surface changes like clothing and dancing, but the manner in which the US was providing a political model for the Chinese dissidents. 'I love an American girl', someone wrote in a Democracy Wall poster, 'her name is democracy.' Other writers challenged the legitimacy of the party dictatorship and suggested that the party monopoly of power had to be demolished in the interest of 'socialist democracy'. There were several views on how the political system could ensure the people's control of government: popular elections, a 'multi-party socialist republic', established laws to protect human rights, Paris Commune style councils, a free press, and so on. It was manifestly clear from their writings that the dissidents had a confused notion of the imported concept of 'democracy', but it was equally clear that they used the term to denounce the past's ultra-left policies, to demand that they be given greater freedom to express their views and to insist that the state be restructured to better protect the rights of the citizens.

The twenty-eight-year-old Wei Jingsheng, who was later arrested for his outspoken comments and who became a symbol of the 'democracy movement', can be taken as a worthy representative of the dissidents. Wei came into prominence for his poster on 'The Fifth Modernization—Democracy', in which he questioned the motives of the Pragmatists and warned the people that the 'Four Modernizations' programme would not liberate them from their thraldom to the party unless the programme was accompanied by democracy. Roger Garside, a British diplomat posted to Beijing, met Wei and got a first-hand account of why Wei had turned against the party.* Wei's alienation began at the age of sixteen, when, as a participant in the Cultural Revolution, he had an opportunity to visit provinces in the hinterland and witness the poverty in the countryside.

> When our train stopped in the Gansu Corridor, a woman with a dirty face and long, loose hair came forward in a group of beggars . . . . I leaned out of the window (of my compartment) to hold out a few buns, but instantly fell back, because I saw something I could never have imagined: the woman with long, loose hair was a girl of eighteen and her body was naked . . . . the sight of the girl haunted me constantly . . . making me search for the cause of her suffering . . . .
>
> Why did such things exist? Were they caused by people disobeying Mao Zedong's instructions? If so, why did he always trust people who disobeyed his instructions? . . .
>
> When (my) early zeal subsided, a question began to form in (my) mind: 'If all power-holders are bad, doesn't that mean the state and party are bad also? . . .'
>
> I know very little of capitalist countries, but now when I see newspaper articles describing the 'superiority of socialism over capitalism', I curse in my heart, saying 'Go to Hell!' The books I have read say that capitalism is bad, but could anything be worse than what I have seen?

* See his fascinating book, *Coming Alive: China After Mao* , McGraw-Hill, 1981.

By March 1979, Deng Xiaoping had come to the conclusion that he no longer needed the dissidents to expose his political enemies; in fact, the activities of the dissidents were becoming counter-productive. In a speech delivered in mid-March, Deng remarked that some people were using the pretext of democracy to foment resentment against the party and its leadership, and that they were making contacts with foreigners and establishing conspiratorial groups. Deng warned the seekers of 'ultra-democracy' that liberalization did not mean that the Chinese who 'danced with the foreigners and sold them secrets' would go unpunished. In a reversal of his 1978 speech, Deng declared that, 'As to the so-called democracy wall and demonstrations and sit-ins, they cannot represent the genuine feelings of our people.'

Deng also announced in his speech the 'Four Cardinal Principles' that made it obligatory for all Chinese unquestioningly to uphold the leadership of the CCP and uphold Marxism–Leninism–Mao Zedong Thought. The principles, which in Deng's own words, 'boiled down to upholding socialism and upholding the party's leadership', were to become the guiding ideology of post-Mao China. The four cardinal principles were written into the party and state constitutions in 1982.

Following Deng's speech, the authorities placed a ban on all posters that were 'opposed to socialism and the leadership of the CCP', and a newspaper in Shanghai reported that, 'Of late, there have been some people who have specialized in hanging around the entrances of hotels and places of entertainment used by the foreigners, telling foreigners erroneous things which distort reality, and taking all sorts of servile attitudes, thus seriously damaging the national self-respect a Chinese person should have.'

On 25 March, Wei Jingsheng put up a poster entitled 'Do We Want Democracy or New Dictatorship?' in which he attacked Deng for turning into a dictator. On 29 March, Wei was arrested. Brought to trial six months later (the proceedings lasted for several hours; there was no defence lawyer and no defence witnesses), he was indicted as a 'counterrevolutionary' who had supplied 'a foreigner (supposedly the Reuter's correspondent) with military intelligence', and had conducted 'counterrevolutionary agitation and propaganda'. Wei was sentenced to fifteen years in jail.

Along with Wei Jingsheng, and following his arrest, several other activists were arrested, and the Democracy Wall was officially declared out of bounds for poster-writers in December 1979. In February 1980, after the new legal codes purporting to protect individual rights had come into effect (1 January 1980), the clause in the 1978 constitution guaranteeing the citizens the right to 'speak out freely, air their views freely, hold great debates and write big-character posters' was repealed. This made poster writing illegal. Similarly, the publication of unofficial journals, under increasing restrictions through 1980, was declared illegal in 1981, and many of the magazine editors were arrested. The so-called democracy movement had been brought to an end.

Deng's declining need for dissident backing ended wholly in 1981, when a pro-Deng Politburo forced Hua Guofeng to resign from the chairmanships of the party and the Central Military Commission (CMC); Hu Yaobang, a protégé of Deng Xiaoping, was elected party chairman (the post was later converted to general secretary), and Deng Xiaoping took over the chairmanship of CMC. Since Hua had already been replaced as prime minister in 1980 by Zhao Ziyang, another Deng protégé, the new reshuffle spelled the end of the Hua era. Deng had a very clear idea of how he wanted to reform China and modernize it; his plans did not include the fissiparous activities of the impractical dissidents. Deng himself would bring socialist democracy and socialist legality to China.

But the genie released in 1978 could not be put back in the shattered bottle of ideology. Indeed, the liberalization that accompanied Deng's reform programmes further weakened what little control ideology could have exerted and encouraged factional infighting in the party, in which the Radical Reformers themselves took up some of the key issues raised by the dissidents.

Deng's Revolutionary Reform Programme: 1980–88

Deng Xiaoping has correctly described his dynamic reform programme, and the massive changes it has brought to China, as 'the second revolution'. At the heart of this revolution are the economic reforms that have shifted China away from both the Maoist model (emphasizing collectivism, egalitarianism and ideological incentives) and the Soviet model (emphasizing the role of centralized state planning, centralized state control and centralized administration of the economy). During the eight years under consideration, Deng succeeded in moving China in the direction of a more diversified economic system that included elements of market economy and new forms of public and private ownership. But because of his political background and commitment to communism, Deng could not accept the emergence of a more pluralistic political order that was called for by his economic policies. The consequence of this lack of balance exploded in the Tiananmen Massacre in 1989 and drove Deng to revive the Maoist emphasis on ideology as an instrument of social control.

Factions: There is no doubt that for nearly a decade Deng has been the Supreme Leader. But, as suggested earlier, Deng has not been able to acquire absolute power and has had to balance various factional interests to keep his policies from collapsing. Broadly speaking, post-Mao China can be said to have two factions and one arbiter: the 'Conservatives', who believe that the Reformers should not go too far in dismantling the socialist policies and structures left behind by Mao; the 'Reformers', who want to 'modernize Marxism' to facilitate Western-style economic modernization; and Deng Xiaoping, the 'faction of one', who is the arbiter. The factional situation is actually far more complicated because the Conservatives include the PLA (in which the Maoist tradition runs deep), the Party Elders (who have been shunted aside by Deng, but who as members of the newly created Central Advisory Commission continue to exert their views), and the Ultra-leftists (Maoist ideologues); similarly, the Reformers include the Radical Reformers (the most Westernized wing of the reform group), the Gradualists (who want China to modernize but who also want to protect socialism by retaining elements of central planning and central control), the Enterpreneurs (an infant class that is out to make profits by using advanced Western business techniques), and the Dissident Intellectuals (professors like Fang Lizhi, who support total Westernization). For our purposes, it will suffice to use the broad categories of 'Conservatives' and 'Reformers', though on occasion reference will be made to the more discrete, smaller groups.

Economic Reforms

The record of economic achievement in the Maoist era was by no means unimpressive. The overall growth rate between 1952 and 1975 was 11.5 per cent in industry and 3.1 per cent in agriculture, which exceeded that of India by a wide margin. And this was achieved without any huge foreign aid or by incurring foreign debts. But this accomplishment was marred by Mao's attempt to create a socialist society at the expense of steady economic growth. The social upheavals created by Mao during the Great Leap Forward and the Cultural Revolution not only retarded economic growth, but saw the return of famine and hunger in the countryside. By the end of his life, Mao had failed to establish a definable economic system and left the populace exhausted and politically disillusioned.

By 1976, China had established a strong industrial base that could facilitate the industrial modernization of the country, but the growth in industry had been sustained by heavy investment squeezed out of the countryside (by keeping procurement prices arbitrarily low) and by denying the workers improvement in living standards; capital accumulation remained high because the masses had few consumer goods to buy. Mao's oft-repeated declaration that the party must serve the masses was an empty slogan that meant precious little to a people whose material needs remained unfulfilled. Indeed, the average grain consumption in the countryside was lower in 1979 than in 1957. It is not surprising, therefore, that labour productivity had begun to decline in the 1970s.

In restructuring the economy, the Reformers discarded Mao's emphasis on ideology and class struggle and shifted to a more pragmatic, profit-oriented approach. One of the most radical changes attempted by the Reformers was in the area of state control over production and pricing. Except for national interest commodities, such as energy and steel, the Reformers tried to reduce state controls and mandatory planning, replacing them with the market. Their hope was that by using indirect levers, such as bank loans on favourable terms for profitable ventures or denial of loans to an inefficient economic unit, the state could guide growth but leave the distribution of commodities and their pricing to market forces.

However, except for the field of agriculture, the reforms were slow in taking hold and had achieved only partial success when the 1989 Tiananmen Massacre brought a reversal of policies and a return to command-style central planning for at least some time to come.

Agricultural Reforms

While the pre-Tiananmen massacre urban and industrial reforms were still 'at a transitional stage', the success of the reforms in agriculture was phenomenal. The Reformers moved quickly to attack the over-concentration of authority in management and improve farm incentives so that living standards in the countryside could be improved. By 1982, the communes, where economic and political authority was concentrated, were being disbanded and agricultural production de-collectivized with the introduction of the 'household responsibility system (HRS)'. The HRS allowed a household (an individual family unit) long-term use of a piece of land in return for the responsibility of paying a fixed amount as tax ('rent').The household was given the right to sell the surplus left over after paying tax in the open market. A significant increase in the state procurement prices of agricultural commodities, and the opportunity to sell their surplus in the open market where the prices were even higher than the procurement prices, had the prompt effect of motivating the peasants to maximize their production. By the end of 1983, the system had spread throughout the country.

Many households that had the expertise managed to accumulate such high profits that they began to invest heavily in chemical fertilizers and in farm machinery. As a consequence of these actions, their incomes increased even more; the party encouraged this development by lauding the success of the outstanding households that had earned 10,000 *yuan* (about $5,000, or 70,000 rupees; the annual *per capita* income in China in 1987 was about 500 *yuan*) in one year, holding them up as models for the others to follow. Such households were even allowed to hire labour and buy trucks and tractors.

The Reformers then went on to invite peasant households to contract 'forests, orchards, tea plantations, mulberry groves, fishponds, livestock' and so on from the collective and to undertake 'specialized' production of certain discrete commodities. The Reformers also urged them to get involved in specialized undertakings, such as 'raising chickens, ducks, rabbits, pigs, or cows, as well as weaving, processing, transportation, repair, service, and commerce'. By 1984, twenty-five per cent of the agricultural labour was involved in highly lucrative non-agricultural work.

The profit motive showed remarkable results, and the gross annual agricultural output value grew from 140 billion *yuan* in 1980 to 587 billion *yuan* in 1988. Although some of the rural areas have not done as well as others, there has been a considerable rise in the living standard of most peasant households, symbolized by the acquisition of radios, TVs, bicycles and sewing machines; in some cases the newly-rich peasants have built impressive private houses and acquired trucks and tractors. This consumerism in turn has led to the expansion of service, and other rural industries and the growth of rural towns that help to absorb unemployed or semi-employed rural labour. Estimates are that nearly a 100 million people are currently employed in collective rural enterprises.

However, agricultural reforms also created certain problems and contributed to certain political controversies. One of the major problems that emerged quite early was connected with the new price control system: the state subsidized the peasantry by paying procurement prices that were higher than what the state charged urban consumers for the same commodities. This became a drain on the national treasury, but when the state tried to solve this problem by not buying grain in excess of the tax amount (hoping that the rest of it would appear in the open market, although at a higher price), the peasants stopped growing extra grain and turned to other, more profitable, cash crops. The percentage of agricultural land used for growing food grains fell from 80.3 per cent in 1978 to 78.3 per cent in 1988; that for cash crops rose from 9.6 per cent to 13.4 per cent.

This had a negative impact on fixed-wage earners in the cities because the free market forces, reflecting the value of certain scarce commodities (such as pork—pigs are raised on grain, and grain was in short supply), drove their prices up to an unacceptable degree. The cost-of-living index for staff and workers in 1988 was 172 per cent higher than in 1980.

While this turn of affairs had a serious enough implication for the leaders who could not afford to lose their popularity among the urban citizenry, they were even more concerned with the possibility that China might not be able to feed its population. Memory of the imperialist days made them fearful that if China were driven to importing grain, it would become dependent on the capitalist world for this essential commodity. As a result, they had to re-apply some central planning controls on the countryside. Yet, in spite of all their attempts to encourage the farmers to shift back to grain, the country failed to reach the declared targets set for grain production. The record grain harvest of 1984, 407 million tons, has not been matched yet; the production figure for 1988 fell to 394 million tons.

Another continuing problem is the household contract system itself. Since all land belongs to the state, and the peasants only have the right of its use for fifteen or so years, there is a natural tendency among the farmers to invest as little as possible capital in the land, and try to get as much as they can out of it in the short term because of the possibility that land might be taken back by the state. Another contradiction inherent in the HCS is that the impressive growth in agriculture is bound to reach a plateau as the limited size of the contracted plots becomes counterproductive. When this happens, as it soon will, the leadership will have to face a fundamental question: should ownership of land be made truly private and richer peasants allowed to increase their holdings by buying out the poorer peasants, or should land be taken back so that large mechanized farms (mechanization is difficult to bring to small holdings) can be established? The leaders would then be faced with an issue that has a direct bearing on the political ideology of the state. Should they allow capitalism to return to the countryside (which can happen only if the country as a whole goes capitalist)? Or should they protect socialism by halting the current trend that is making some areas (those that are more fertile and better irrigated) and some households (those with more capital and expertise) richer? To decide in favour of the latter course would put the leadership in a dilemma because the state has actually decreased its investment in agriculture, instead depending heavily on the richer areas and richer peasants to maintain the momentum of agricultural growth.

The major changes that have taken place in the agricultural sector pose serious questions for a state that professes to be socialistic: the new policies have not only conspicuously increased the disparities in rural incomes, putting the small percentage of rich households far ahead of the others, but have actually made the poorer, disadvantaged peasants even poorer. In 1985, it was estimated that eight per cent of the rural population (70,000,000 persons) was living in poverty and was in dire need of help. The figure has increased since then.

Another side effect of the agricultural reforms, and their success, has been the increase in the rural birth rate. In 1980, the Reformers adopted 'a one child per family' policy, which has been carried out quite harshly ever since. However, the economic utility of male children in intensive farming, which depends largely on muscle power, tended to undermine the one-child policy in the countryside. The richer households flouted the policy because they could afford to pay the fines and forsake the incentives offered by the state. This put the leaders in a quandary because to punish these households (for example, by selling less fertilizer to them) the Reformers would have to take away the very incentives they were otherwise offering in the interest of higher production. On a broader level, one tragic outcome of the one-child policy has been an increase in female infanticide.

Industrial and Commercial Reforms

If one looks at statistical figures and indices, China's performance in the arena of urban economics from 1980 to 1988 has been very good, even spectacular. The average annual increase in the value of gross industrial output during this period has been 12.8 per cent. However, unlike the more consistent success in the agricultural field, the performance in the urban sector has been subject to fluctuations and swings that have required constant readjustment.

From 1979 to 1984, the period of 're-adjustment, restructuring, and consolidation', tentative efforts were made to reduce the over-concentration of economic power in the hands of the state authorities and transfer decision-making power to the industrial enterprises. The new policies were premised on the consideration that since the 1,000,000 urban enterprises (industrial, building, transport, commercial and service; with a work force of 80,000,000 and contributing eighty per cent of the state revenues) were directly responsible for industrial production, they should be revitalized by being made more autonomous. The popular socialist concept that *ownership* of the enterprises by the whole people (which actually means ownership by the 'state') in effect meant *direct operation* of the enterprises by the state. Now direct control had to be discarded and the enterprises allowed to 'plan their own production, supply and marketing; keep and budget funds they are entitled to retain; appoint, remove employ or elect their own personnel . . . ; decide on how to recruit and use their own work force, and on wages and rewards; set the prices of their products within the limits prescribed by the state; and so on.' However, the state could continue to manage, inspect, guide and regulate the activities of the enterprises 'through planning and by economic, administrative and legal means'.

In brief, the reforms were aimed at bringing the 'economic responsibility system'(as a counterpart to what had been done in the countryside), to urban enterprises by making them more independent. The programme to restructure industrial and commercial enterprises was gradually introduced by allowing a certain number of them to have some say in planning, in purchasing and marketing products, in the use of funds (areas totally dominated earlier by centralized authorities) and in the appointment and dismissal of intermediate level managerial staff. By 1984, many of these enterprises were able to retain a share of the profits instead of handing them all over to the state as they had done earlier; they now paid 'taxes'. The funds retained were used for compensating efficient workers with bonuses, for capital investment, and for improving workers' housing, etc.

In 1984, the Reformers went a step further by announcing new changes that were aimed at establishing a 'socialist planned commodity economy with Chinese characteristics'. This meant that the reforms, while re-emphasizing the need for the enterprises to have greater freedom in decision-making, aimed to push China towards a more open market by freeing some pricing from central control. But the efforts of the Reformers to restructure the industrial sector ran into difficulties because of the patchwork fashion in which the devolution of central controls was taking place. Power could not be shifted wholly from the hands of the entrenched party and state bureaucracy to that of the managers of economic units till price reform (which alone could ensure the establishment of a free market) had been carried out fully. Policies that allowed some prices to fluctuate while keeping others fixed did not establish the infrastructure required for market forces to work freely. Furthermore, in China's resource-hungry economy with its captive market, the establishment of floating prices led to widespread corruption and price fixing. It also resulted in double-digit inflation that eroded the purchasing power of urban wage earners. This was a politically sensitive issue, and the rapid rise in the retail prices of daily-use commodities would become one of the causes behind the 1989 'democracy movement'.

Also, the deeply ingrained attitudes of socialist egalitarianism among the working class (equal wages and no firing of unneeded or inefficient workers), a legacy of the Maoist era, thwarted the managers from attaining the efficiency desired by the new programmes. Furthermore, the conflict of interest between the locality and the province, the province and the centre, was another obstacle in the path of economic modernization; for example, less efficient rural enterprises, because they were protected by local authorities, could not be eliminated by the capital-rich, efficient urban units. Similarly, provincial governments provided support and protection for their provincial enterprises even if they were less competitive than similar enterprises in other provinces or enterprises under central control.

The top-heavy state administration, with its many vested interests and a proclivity to interfere in the organizational work of the enterprises, also was reluctant to give up power. Its unscrupulous behaviour was possible because the policies that supposedly transferred authority to the managers were not clear-cut on the issue of responsibility. The Reformers, who appear to have thought about everything else, had overlooked the need for a concerted effort to restructure the Chinese bureaucracy, which had doubled between 1978 and 1988.

The situation was confounded by infighting between the factions; the Radical Reformers believed that the modernization programme could only succeed if market-oriented reforms were pushed further and a shift made from public to private ownership; the Conservatives felt that the economic order, destabilized by the forces unleashed with the market-oriented reforms and the rampant inflation that had followed, could be restored only by bringing back centralized state controls. More moderate opinion supported the reforms as long as they did not encourage privatization or capitalism.

The trouble with the moderate view, which did offer a workable compromise solution, was not that a mixed economy was impossible to achieve. (India, for example, has developed this kind of economy in which public and private ownership coexist with market mechanisms.) The trouble was that China had no experience with such an economy and had proceeded too rapidly without laying the proper foundation for its development. Without a free market to exercise discipline, the enterprises, with their increased autonomy, maximized investment to carry out uncontrolled capital construction (building houses and enlarging factories) which outstripped industrial output. Accompanied by an expansion in money supply, easy credits, growth of national deficits, and an increase in foreign debt, this resulted in lowering labour productivity and 'heating' the economy. The average urban Chinese household had to bear the brunt of this maladjusted economy with the runaway inflation that followed. In the absence of constructive economic thinking, the entire economy came unglued in late 1988/early 1989, and the Tiananmen Massacre brought to a close the first phase of economic reforms. Since then, the leaders have reverted to a combination of command economy and tight fiscal programmes.

As one noted Chinese economist, Liu Guoguang, summed it up in April 1989:

> Taking the leap between the old and the new ways has much to do with the causes of this economic disorder . . . . .
>
> We should change the state of things in which the new and old

systems co-exist while understanding that reforms . . . are a long way from completion . . . .

Since the start of the reform period in late 1978, the nation has actually progressed through two stages. During the first few years people generally agreed that a relaxed economic environment was required. A 'buyers market'—that is an economic condition when *supply* slightly exceeds *demand*—predominated. It was believed that such a system would bring into play market forces that would spur reform and development.

But this view was dropped by the end of 1984 when the Chinese found themselves in the grips of inflation. A new way of thinking predominated which held that reform could only be carried through when *demand* would be allowed to outstrip *supply* . . . People at all levels wished to record higher output statistics. Soon excessive development targets sent the demand rates soaring well beyond the supply level. Investments expanded, with many production lines imported . . . .

China is facing a big paradox with its present restraint programme.

No one wants to tighten up, but if we give in, inflation will go further beyond control and with the public anticipating even greater increases, the entire economy will break down.

Before leaving the subject of urban reform policies, two other areas of change require brief notice: private and collective ownership, and the role of foreign capital.

The reforms had encouraged the establishment of collectively and privately owned enterprises, which were far more autonomous by their very nature than state enterprises. Though the private enterprises are on a very small scale, mostly in the area of repair workshops, tailoring, restaurants, retail stores, and service trades, they have absorbed millions of the urban unemployed and enlivened the local economic scene. The collectively-owned urban enterprises are much larger, operating hotels and running companies that deal with service and trade industries. Because they bring attractive profits, ministries of the central government, various state and party organizations, and even universities and colleges have got into the act. Since 'important' people are associated with them, these enterprises manage to obtain investment funding and licenses to import luxury consumer goods. The consequent corruption engendered by the collectively-owned enterprises has become the cause of much popular criticism.

One of the unique developments in post-Mao China has been the opening of the country to foreign entrepreneurs who have been encouraged to establish enterprises which are wholly underwritten by foreign private capital, joint ventures, and projects based on compensation trade (the Chinese build the factories and provide cheap labour to foreign entrepreneurs who bring in the machinery and technology; the profits earned by the export of the items produced are used to compensate the foreign businessmen). Special Economic Zones (SEZs), isolated from the internal market, have been set up near several ports to attract foreign businesses by offering them favourable taxes and easy profit repatriation facilities. By mid-1989 China had approved 18,000 foreign-backed businesses, with contractual investments exceeding thirty billion US dollars. Though the funds 'actually utilized' were far less than this amount, there has been a significant input from abroad, and some of the great international business houses, such as Mitsui, IBM, Volkswagen, and Coca Cola, are now operating in China.

The use of foreign capital has helped China in several major projects, such as oil exploration, coal mining, construction of thermal power units, and establishment of factories to manufacture cars and trucks, film and photographic equipment, chemical fertilizers and optical fibres. Twenty-one billion dollars (US) of foreign capital has been used by China to buy 5,000 items of advanced technology. This has helped modernize consumer-goods industries, ranging from telephone switch-boards to computer-controlled elevators. Foreign funds have also helped modernize twenty-five per cent of the rural enterprises and build a hundred luxury hotels; Sino-foreign joint ventures have created over 2,000,000 jobs in the cities and the countryside. Apart from modernizing China's industrial infrastructure, the export of commodities produced by foreign-funded enterprises has contributed to an expansion of exports; in 1988, the value of these exports was approximately 2.5 billion dollars.

However, the hope that foreign collaboration would help the country by providing a training ground for management and personnel has not quite worked out because foreign enterprises are unwilling to run training workshops for staff they do not need. Foreign enterprises, finding that staff allocated by the Chinese authorities did not meet their requirements, have, in some cases, got permission to hire directly. This has had a disturbing result: many highly-educated and over-qualified persons apply for lowly positions because they are better paying than many other jobs. One foreign hotel manager in Shanghai, for example, was flooded by applications from graduate and post-graduate students to fill the few openings he had advertised for waiters and chamber maids. Foreigners have also noted that Chinese management personnel, however well-trained in foreign-style modern management techniques, still find it difficult to overcome their psychological inhibitions against dismissing workers for incompetence.

Dealings with foreign businesses and contact with foreign trade have also accentuated the traditional Chinese penchant for bribes and corruption. Party and government cadres who are linked with organizations dealing with foreigners thrive on kickbacks and illegal dealings in foreign exchange. Chinese newspapers often carry stories of cadres who have profited from their official positions in many devious ways. In 1985, for example, Hainan Island produced a scandal of unbelievable proportions that shocked the entire country. The Hainan party committee used its foreign-exchange allocation to import (tax-free) hundreds of thousands of colour television sets, video cassette recorders, motor cycles and 89,000 motor vehicles. It then proceeded to sell these goods to other provinces at double or triple the original prices, sharing the gains with the entire population of Hainan! Yet all this was done within the legal parameters set by the state.

Two other policies advocated by the Reformers, concerning family planning and education, also require attention.

Family Planning

Mao's belief that human labour was China's most important asset had resulted in the neglect of family planning after 1958. When they were in power between 1959 and 1965, the Pragmatists attempted to activate family planning programs, but without much success. Only at the end of the Great Proletarian Cultural Revolution did Mao change his mind and authorize a nationwide campaign for family planning. The rationale behind the campaign was that a socialist country with a planned economic development required parallel planned population growth. The proposition was put rather starkly by the Chinese delegate to the World Population Conference in 1974: 'We do not approve of anarchy, either in material production or in human reproduction.'

Chinese economic planners called for an overall population growth of one per cent by 1980, 0.5 per cent by 1985, and zero growth by 1900. The immediate target of the government was summed up in the slogan, 'One (child) is good, two are all right, three are too many.' Propaganda, group pressure, and negative incentives helped bring down the birth rate to 1.2 per cent by 1976. However, after Mao had passed from the scene, the new leaders, who viewed the matter far more seriously, introduced in 1978 a clause in the constitution that 'the state advocates and encourages family planning'. This provided a legal base to what so far had been merely administrative regulations. In a ruthlessly cold and calculated fashion, a policy that made it illegal for a family to have more than one child was then launched.

The state used both administrative coercion and material incentives in its campaign to spread the new doctrine. It offered as an incentive to married couples who had only one child, free health care for the child, as well as monetary rewards, extra workpoints (which meant a higher income) and extra pensions for the parents when they retired (so that the state, instead of sons, would provide them security in old age). The couples were also promised favourable consideration in the allocation of good jobs and better housing. There were also 'negative incentives': a couple that insisted on having several children was not only denied the rewards given to a one-child family, but was taxed for each extra child. Naturally, the one-child policy was extremely unpopular, particularly in rural China, for it went against deeply entrenched traditional family values.

In the first few years of the campaign, administrative coercion played a more important role than material incentives. Over-zealous cadres, intent on keeping the number of children born in their area of jurisdiction within the officially-allocated quota, used draconian methods to ensure results. They held meetings in factories and other collective groups to decide which of the married women in the group could have a child in the following year and which had to postpone plans for a family till the party gave permission. Afraid of being penalized for not meeting targets, cadres harassed and humiliated women who had become pregnant out of turn or had become pregnant for the second time. Water and electricity were often cut off from the living quarters of the errant family till the pregnant woman agreed to an abortion. In many communes, pregnant women were 'arrested' and taken away in handcuffs for having committed the 'crime' of having become 'illegally' pregnant. In 1983, the government actually ordered sterilization for all couples with two children and abortions for all unauthorized pregnancies.

The one-child policy has generally been more successful in the cities than in the villages. Though newly-married city couples usually make more money than their counterparts in the villages, the life of the urbanites is much harder. Typically allocated a one-room apartment, they have to share bathroom and cooking facilities with other residents in the building. Normally, both men and women work six days a week, but in addition to working eight hours a day, they often must spend several hours commuting and standing in queues to buy meat and other rationed articles of daily use. These couples tend to postpone having a child till they get better housing, by which time they have usually succumbed to various administrative and social pressures and have accepted the notion that one child is enough.

Conditions in the countryside are different. Peasant families, even the poorer ones, usually live in self-contained housing units and lead 'freer' lives, far less constricted than those of their urban counterparts; administrative dis-incentives do not carry the same weight in the countryside as they do in the cities. The desire for children among the peasantry is also greater because children are needed to help in farming activities and as security in old age; the state does not yet have the resources to establish a national pension system for the countryside. Local cadres, not wanting to antagonize the people with whom they have to live, now often do not push hard to implement the one-child policy. But in the early years, where they did do so and were successful in their efforts, a rash of female infanticides resulted because the peasants wanted a son rather than a daughter as their only child.

After a period of coercive action (forced sterilizations, IUD insertions, and abortions), which created widespread internal opposition to the government, the leaders moderated their policies in 1984. They were, no doubt, also influenced to some degree (notwithstanding their public denials) by strong opposition to draconian Chinese family-planning practices in the outside world, particularly in the United States. A US Senate subcommittee heard testimony on the issue in 1984, and in 1985 America decided to withhold $10,000,000 from its contribution to the United Nations Fund for Population Activities, a sum that was equal to the amount UNFPA spent annually in China. Some Chinese analysts, too, began to suggest that any sudden change in the population growth would lead to a rapid ageing of the Chinese population, exacerbating the problem of financial security for the retirees. Another social cost also needed to be considered: the one child in a family, doted upon by parents and grandparents and a recipient of many privileges from the state, tended to become spoiled, self-centred, stubborn, selfish, and disrespectful.

After 1985, the population goal for the year 2000 was slightly amended to permit a more flexible approach. This resulted in a rise in the birth rate, which is expected to exceed twenty-one per thousand in 1989, and the matter currently has become a cause of increased worry for the leaders. Speaking at the National Conference on Family Planning Publicity in October 1989, the Minister of the State Planning Commission emphasized the need for making greater efforts 'to publicize the importance of family planning' because in some rural areas families were allowed 'to have a second child if their first was a girl'. The minister said that though education should be given top priority, 'administrative, legal, and economic measures should be adopted to make sure people comply with the national programme'. One wonders if another harsh campaign is in the offing.

Education

Though the quantitative growth of student numbers and educational facilities was dramatic from 1949 to 1976, educational development in the Maoist era was erratic and suffered repeated setbacks. As a result, despite all efforts by the Reformers, China has yet to catch up with India (another large Asian country to which China can be compared) in the field of higher education. In 1988, the relative placement of students in the two countries was as follows:

	China	*India*
Primary	128.4 m	129.2 m
Secondary	54.0 m	20.1 m
University	2.0 m	3.8 m

The contrast is even more striking when one bears in mind that China's population in 1988 was over one billion as against India's 800 plus million.

The Reformers tried to rectify the deficiencies created by Maoist policies toward education by promulgating a series of reforms that were intended to ensure that, over a period of time, Chinese children would have nine years compulsory schooling and that primary school students would have easier access to technical and vocational schools. More importantly, to satisfy the demands of the modernization drive, the reforms conceded greater autonomy to universities and colleges in the areas of admission and curriculum planning, and in the development of post graduate and research fields. The reforms also encouraged institutes of higher learning to establish links with foreign countries and liberalized policies governing the sending of students abroad for specialized studies.

The desire of the Reformers to bring China on par with the most advanced countries in the realm of science and technology is represented by the large number of students and scholars sent to Japan and the Western states. The favoured country is the United States, which issued 75,800 student and scholar-exchange visas from 1 January 1979 to 30 September 1988 (the number increased to 80,000 by the spring of 1989). Available figures for students sent to the other countries from 1978 to 1984 are (approximately): 3,900 to Japan, 2,500 to West Germany (till 1986), 1,800 to Britain, 1,300 to France, 1,452 to Canada. When Deng Xiaoping accepted plans for Chinese students to study abroad, he was aware that some might choose not to come back. However, he was confident that the majority would return to help in the modernization programmes. Deng had also calculated that the risk involved in the students returning with their minds 'contaminated' with Western political and social ideals was containable, and he managed to dilute the Conservatives' reaction against the 'spiritual pollution' that was introduced into the country through the openness to the West. But he could not have foreseen the response of the students abroad to the Tiananmen Massacre and their massive outpouring of criticism against the Chinese government. Today it is doubtful how many of them will return home to be punished for their 'unpatriotic' stand. Of the 51,000 students in the States, 11,000 have already become 'permanent residents', and many of the other 40,000 are also likely to seek a change of visa status.

Internally, the new educational policies have so far met with mixed success: education has advanced more rapidly in the cities than in the countryside; the richer areas in the countryside have established more primary schools than the poorer ones; the Household Contract System has actually led to a withdrawal of students from primary schools because they are needed in the family enterprise; the growth in the number of 'technical schools' gives a false sense of promise—many of the old schools have merely changed their names without changing the content of the education they offer; there is a shortage of trained teachers, and many schools have unqualified teaching staff; the children of high party and state cadres manage to go to the best schools and universities, thereby widening the already-existing gap between elite and non-elite institutions.

The most unsatisfactory aspect of the reform policies is that the financial burden of schooling is being shifted from the state to the collectives and to private individuals. This may be in keeping with the other economic policies that aim to withdraw the state from direct participation in various enterprises, but it has many negative ramifications. Some of the poorer collectives in the countryside have been forced to close down primary schools. Even in the cities, the universities have begun to favour tuition-paying students, and since the tuition charged is often more than the average annual income of a worker, the children of the rich, however competitively unqualified, gain entrance at the expense of bright, but poor, students. In the absence of adequate state subsidies, colleges and universities have not been able to appreciably raise the salaries of the teachers (one of the complaints of the students in the Tiananmen demonstrations in 1989). The students, too, have suffered from benign neglect: living six to a dormitory room, eating unappetizing institutional food, and receiving their education in classrooms in need of renovation and laboratories in need of equipment. To sum up, the quantitative expansion in education has not yet been paralleled to the extent desirable by a qualitative improvement.

The Politics of Reform and 'Democracy'

The 'two lines' in developmental policy that emerged in 1959, representing the Maoists and the Liuists, were replicated, in a manner of speaking, in the Deng era by the factional competition between the Moderate Reformers and the Radical Reformers. The Moderates hoped to keep a firm control over the reform programmes and not allow them to undermine the political structure and ideology of the state as it had evolved through 1976; the Radicals, on the other hand, saw the reforms as having a vitality and a direction of their own, which they felt should be given free play and not be thwarted by artificial barriers. The Moderate Reformers often found support among the Conservatives, while the Radical Reformers received the backing of the intellectuals and the students. To simplify, at this stage we will use the umbrella term 'Reformers' for the Radical Reformers, while 'Conservatives' (sometimes also referred to as 'Reactionaries') will signify all the other factions, including the Moderate Reformers.

In the tensions and conflict that marked the relationship between the Reformers and the Conservatives, Deng Xiaoping's position was far from clear cut. There was never any doubt that Deng stood firmly for economic modernization, but he also maintained that he was committed to keeping China solidly on the path of socialism and never allowing the role of the party to be undermined. In practice this meant that Deng was constrained periodically to put curbs on the Radical Reformers whenever their policies tended to reduce the role of the party or push China too far from the path of orthodox socialism. Similarly, Deng had to restrain the Conservatives at other times when he found that their Leftist views stood in the way of economic liberalization. In other words, Deng tried to steer a difficult course between leftist and rightist influences. And this has seriously influenced the leadership succession problem.

By the time our story ends, in the months following the Spring Massacre of 1989, a beleaguered Deng was trying to salvage his modernization programmes by sacrificing the chief Reformers, his protégés, and yielding to the demands of the Conservatives. Deng's troubles can be traced to the very beginning of the modernization drive,when he put forward the idea that political relaxation and the down-playing of ideology were necessary to carry out reforms. Although it was never his intention to let 'bourgeois liberalism' creep into the country, the reforms fostered a milieu that favoured increasing liberalization of the political system. Unfortunately for Deng, the weakening of Maoist ideological appeals, coupled with the rise of consumerism and a materialistic culture, brought corruption and nepotism in the wake of profit-oriented economic policies, confused the issue of 'modernization' and gave the Conservatives a handle to attack the Reformers and their policies. The Conservatives also related the break-down of social discipline, and the consequent rise of social crimes (prostitution, bank robberies, thefts, etc.), to the erosion of socialist values created by the opening of China to the West. In the eyes of the Conservatives, 'Socialist' China could not afford to pay such a high cost for economic modernization. Deng's predicament was created by the fact that he could neither eliminate the Conservatives nor put curbs on the excessive exuberance of the Reformers. From 1981 (after he had suppressed the dissident intellectuals and the so-called student 'democracy movement') to 1983, Deng moved to purge the party of 'three types of people': those who had been followers of the Gang of Four, those who were factionalists, and those who had committed acts of violence during the Great Proletarian Cultural Revolution. Deng's obvious intention was to consolidate his position within the party by eliminating all Conservative opposition capable of thwarting his reform programmes.

However, Deng's anti-left moves were exploited by the Reformers to criticize the old socialist orthodoxy and bolster their liberal policies. They did this by encouraging the publication of articles that took up the themes of 'socialist alienation', 'Marxist humanism', and 'democracy', and by allowing writers to produce 'protest literature' that, under the garb of describing atrocities committed during the Cultural Revolution, attacked the rigidity of party ideology. The Conservatives, particularly the old-timers, viewed this intellectual movement as a by-product of the 'decadent' ideas that were infiltrating China from the outside world. The permissive environment was responsible for fostering the 'spiritual pollution' that was undermining the culture of the entire nation. Was it not the widespread acceptance of liberal, bourgeois ideas that had also led to corruption and nepotism and the popularity of pornographic video tapes and literature which were being smuggled into the country from Hong Kong and the capitalist West? By 1983, the question of 'spiritual pollution' had become a major national issue.

Deng, no doubt as upset over these developments as his other older colleagues, came out openly against 'humanism' and 'alienation' and other elements of so-called decadence. However, Deng's speech in the fall of 1983 indicates his attempt to maintain a position somewhere between the two extremes of the political spectrum:

> The decision on rectification (of the party) lists 'three types of people'. It also mentions people who have committed serious economic or other crimes, people who have abused power for private gains, people who have seriously impaired the party's relations with the masses, people who have been at odds with the party politically all along or who have merely pretended to be in agreement with it, and so forth . . . .
>
> However, quite a few comrades have made only a one-sided analysis of the historical lessons . . . (They) are only interested in

combating 'left' mistakes and not 'right' ones. This leads to the other extreme, weakness and laxity. In waging ideological struggle against negative tendencies, persons and acts, and in metting out organizational sanctions, *party people have tended in recent years to be a little too tolerant, hesitant, tender-hearted and ready to gloss things over to avoid trouble. Party discipline has been so lax that some bad people were shielded* . . . .

Now I come to the second point: people working in the ideological field must not spread spiritual pollution . . . .

All our workers fighting on the ideological front should serve as 'engineers of the soul' . . . . and hold aloft the banner of Marxism and socialism . . . .

A number of theorists are indifferent to the major theoretical questions raised by socialist modernization . . . . They have engaged in discussions of the value of the human being, humanism and alienation and have only been interested in criticizing socialism, not capitalism . . . . It is true that the standards of living and education of our people are not high, but discussion of the value of the human being and of humanism isn't going to raise that. Only active efforts to achieve material, ideological and cultural progress can do that . . . .

(Some) people preach abstract democracy, even advocating free expression of counterrevolutionary views. They set democracy in opposition to party leadership . . .

(Some) writers make a point of writing about the dark side of life, they spread pessimism and sometimes even concoct stories to distort the revolutionary past and present. Others loudly praise the 'modern' schools of thought of the West . . . (A) few produce pornography . . . (And some) stage low and vulgar shows just to make money . . . .

(Some) of our comrades rush to praise to the skies all trends in the philosophy, economics, socio-politics, literature and art of the West, without analyzing them, distinguishing the good from the bad, or exercising any critical judgement . . . .

Spiritual pollution can be so damaging as to bring disaster upon the country and the people. It blurs the distinction between right and wrong, leads to passivity, laxity and disunity, corrupts the mind and erodes the will. It encourages all kinds of individualism and causes people to doubt or even to reject socialism and the party's leadership . . . .

Don't think that a little spiritual pollution doesn't matter much, that it's nothing to be alarmed about. But unless we take it seriously and adopt firm measures right now to prevent its spread, many people will fall prey to it and be led astray, with grave consequences. *In the long run this question will determine what kind of people will succeed us to carry on the cause and what the future of the party and state will be.*

The campaign against 'spiritual pollution' was launched within a few days of Deng's speech, and many party cadres, not quite sure what 'spiritual pollution' actually meant, began to persecute persons across the spectrum, those involved in foreign trade at one end, and those who had fancy hairstyles, used cosmetics or went disco dancing at the other. The campaign appeared to be taking on the dimensions of the Cultural Revolution; it created a crisis that threatened the reforms, damaged the confidence of the intelligentsia in the party leadership and had an adverse impact on China's image abroad. Simultaneously, the government also tried to reduce economic and social crimes by harsh administrative action. Each province was ordered to publicly execute a given number of criminals as a negative example for the others; 10,000 public executions were carried out nationwide. Foreign investors began to have second thoughts about China's Open Door policies because they saw in this campaign a drive to isolate China from the world.

General Secretary Hu Yaobang and Premier Zhao Ziyang, the chief Reformers, persuaded Deng Xiaoping to reverse his judgement, and the campaign was brought to a sudden halt in early 1984. Obviously, Deng could not afford to have his reform programme derailed. He, therefore, also permitted the Reformers to calm the fears of the intelligentsia by reaffirming the Reformers' commitment to providing the intellectuals a liberal environment to work in. These decisions, regardless of how or why they were reached, highlight Deng's dilemma. No doubt, he was sincere in stressing the need for the party to strengthen its ideological controls; but at the same time, he could not afford to permit the re-surfacing of leftist policies. When he talked of ideology, he perforce had to go back to the 'Marxism–Leninism Thought of Mao Zedong'; yet, he could not tolerate the idea of Maoism re-emerging.

Deng's dilemma was aggravated in 1984, when new policies to reform the economic structures in the urban areas were introduced and the goals set for developing a market-oriented commodity economy. Since Marxism opposed commodity production, the Reformers had to find some pretext for revising Marxism and justifying their policies on other grounds. This they did by asserting that Marx's writings, however appropriate they may have been a hundred years ago, could not be expected to solve 'our current problems'. Theoretical defence of the new policies went so far as to declare that Marxism was not a dogma, but a broad guide to action: 'Marx envisaged that under socialism there would be no need for commodities and currency, but our practice of socialist construction has proved that socialist society cannot do without commodities or currency. If we cannot do anything that Marx did not advocate, then what are we to do?' The solution: China must develop its own brand of 'socialism with Chinese characteristics'.

The Conservatives were not convinced by this argument. Even the veteran economic planner, Chen Yun, who fell in the çategory of Moderate Reformer, questioned the growing role of market forces and saw the withdrawal of central controls over the economy as creating 'chaos'. He also linked the new policies to corruption among party leaders at the highest level. 'I hope,' Chen said, 'the party's senior leaders will set a good example by educating their children, who absolutely must not use their parents' positions in pursuing personal power and interests and becoming privileged.' He made a blunt reference to 'some people (who) in their dealings with foreigners have no considerations of personal or national dignity'.

For the common city people, who had little interest in ideological debates, 1984 was the beginning of higher prices and inflation, problems which continue to bother them to this day. Scandals, such as the 'Hainan motor vehicles incident' and press reports of children of high officials involved in robberies and gang rapes, only added to their cynicism and frustration. As far as 'nepotistic' practices were concerned, children of leaders like Deng Xiaoping and Zhao Ziyang were known to have travelled (for studies) abroad before returning to lucrative jobs with the new firms being established because of the Open Door policies. There is little doubt that such discontent fed a deep frustration that exploded in riots at the Beijing stadium in May 1985, when the Chinese national soccer team lost to Hong Kong in the World Cup qualifying match.

By 1986, the Reformers were convinced that many of the perplexing problems generated by the economic reforms could not be resolved till corresponding reforms in the political system were made. Deng, without whose approval nothing could be done, went along with the general idea of political restructuring and announced that reforms should be introduced to 'streamline the administration, delegate real powers to lower levels and broaden the scope of socialist democracy, so as to bring into play the initiative of the masses and the grass-roots organizations'.

The opening provided by Deng Xiaoping was used by Hu Yaobang and Zhao Ziyang to go much further in the direction of liberalization than the limits Deng may have had in mind. Fortuitously, 1986 also marked the thirtieth anniversary of the Hundred Flowers Movement, and Hu Yaobang, the patron of the liberal intellectuals, took the occasion to initiate a full-fledged debate on the essence of Chinese socialism. He proclaimed: 'No advanced philosophical thought should become dogma. It should instead be a spiritual force that incites people to ceaselessly search and create. It should develop in step with the development of actual situations.'

Party and non-party intellectuals rushed in to join the debate, and there was an outpouring of unorthodox ideas that shocked not only the Conservatives, but even the Moderate Reformers. There were calls for 'democratic pluralism' and attacks on the 'incorrect' viewpoint that 'ills that appear in the course of economic reform should be rectified by the construction of spiritual civilization'. China needed a new theoretical basis for its development because 'there is no available experience to copy from for China's reforms'. Marx was condemned for being 'obsolete'.

The most extreme stand was taken by intellectuals who saw no reason for China to fear 'wholesale Westernization'. On the contrary, without a proper understanding of Western political thought and culture, social sciences, educational principles, and ideology, China could not hope to gain a complete knowledge of Western science and technology.

The Reformers used the 'New Hundred Flowers Movement', as the drive for free speech came to be called, very much like Mao had used the movement in 1957. But their objective was different: they were not out to ensnare the 'rightist' intellectuals, but to eliminate the 'leftist' opposition.

The Reformers cleverly even used Marxism to undermine the Maoist ideologues. They accepted Marx's assertion that the economic foundation of society determined social consciousness (culture), only to reverse the argument of the Conservatives that political work must precede economic reform. Their conclusion: nothing should be allowed to hinder economic reform. Premier Zhao Ziyang took up this theme in his announcement of the Seventh Five-Year-Plan in April 1986: 'We must resolutely transform all those ideas, rules and regulations that conflict with the development of a commodity economy.' (Marx, it must be remembered, was against commodity economy.)

The 'free speech' movement brought forth a spate of half-baked ideas on how China could further liberalize its politics. The ideas were exciting, but ultimately they did not provide any coherent formula for reducing the role of the party in national affairs. Indeed, they could not be reconciled with Deng's Four Cardinal Principles. So the old dilemma continued to baffle the Reformers: how to keep the party from usurping the functions of government, the government from usurping the functions of enterprises, and the bureaucracy from guiding all aspects of socialist life. The notion that the judiciary and the legislature should be strengthened to counterbalance the executive was rejected by all senior party members, including Deng. In fact, in September 1986, while re-iterating his nebulous ideas of political restructuring, Deng put a lid on further consideration of Western-style democratic institutions by adding: 'However, in reforming our political structure we must not imitate the West, *and no liberalization should be allowed* . . . (if) we place too much emphasis on checks and balances, problems may arise.' At another forum in the same month, Deng asserted that:

> (Liberalization is) bourgeois in nature—there is no such thing as proletarian or socialist liberalization. Liberalization by itself means antagonism to our current policies and systems and a wish to revise them. In fact the exponents of liberalization want to lead us down the road to capitalism. That is why we call it bourgeois liberalization . . . . It seems to me that the struggle against liberalization will have to be carried on not only now but for the next ten or twenty years. *If we fail to check this trend it will merge with undesirable foreign things that will inevitably find their way into China because of our open policy and become a battering ram used against our modernization programme.*

By November, though he was still talking about reform in the political structure, Deng had shifted his ground to emphasize the need 'to ensure the continuing vitality of the party and the state'. And though still concerned about the overlapping functions of the party and the state, he said: 'We must uphold the leadership of the party, which is one of the characteristics of China, and never abandon it, but the party should exercise its leadership effectively.' He added in a note of frustration: 'It's several years already since we first raised the problem of efficiency, *but we still have no clear idea as to how to solve it.*'

However limited its contribution to political reform, the intellectual environment of open debate, discussion and liberalized thought had a significant impact on the University campuses. The students were also influenced by literature from Hong Kong, and even from Taiwan, brought in by millions of overseas Chinese visiting the homeland. Although student activism periodically had resulted in demonstrations in 1984 and 1985 (for example, demonstrations against Japan for its 'economic invasion' of China), these cases were few in number. In 1986, however, the demonstrations became more widespread and more iconoclastic in nature, reflecting the radical ideas of the Reformers. The most common slogans of the demonstrators were: 'Long Live Democracy', 'We Demand Human Rights', and 'Down With Bureaucratism'. These demonstrations were unauthorized and, therefore, technically 'illegal'.

The great idol of the students was Professor Fang Lizhi, Vice-Chancellor of the University of Science and Technology (UST) in Hefei (capital of Anhui province) and an internationally recognized astro-physicist. Fang believed in wholesale Westernization and inspired his students to fight for democracy because 'democracy must be won, not handed down from above'. Student opinion was also influenced by the fiery speeches of Liu Binyan, a dissident journalist of national standing. There is every reason to believe that both Fang and Liu had the support of Hu Yaobang. Fang visited most of the well-known universities and gave highly provocative speeches extolling the virtues of wholesale Westernization, an example of which may be seen in the following excerpts from a speech delivered at Tong Ji University Shanghai, in November 1986*:

> The system cries out for modernization. But what kind of modernization do we want? The truth is every aspect of the Chinese world needs to be modernized. But do we want to be completely Westernized? No new controversy, this question has been asked for more than a century. *As for myself, I think that complete Westernization is the only way to modernize.* (*enthusiastic applause*) I believe in thorough, comprehensive liberalization because Chinese culture is primitive, not just backward in any particular respect.
>
> There is no reason whatsoever to restrict liberalization before it begins. (*enthusiastic applause*) As I have said the call for complete Westernization is nothing new. The rationale has been the notion that the Western assault upon any particular aspect of Chinese society, be it government, economics, science, technology or education, reflects upon the weakness of Chinese society as a whole . . . But the roots of our backwardness lie in our history. We have changed a lot over the past century, yet we are still far behind the rest of the world. Frankly, I feel we still lag behind because *these decades of socialist experimentation since Liberation have been—well, a failure!* (*long applause*) This is not just my opinion. It is clear to all eyes . . . .

---

* See *China Spring*, Vol. 1, No. 2, March/April 1987.

I am here to tell you that the socialist movement, from Marx and Lenin to Stalin and Mao Zedong, has been a failure. (*enthusiastic applause*)

(It) is important to note that democracy is quite different from relaxation of restrictions. The critical component of the democratic agenda is human rights, a touchy issue in our country. Human rights are fundamental privileges that people have from birth, such as the right to think and be educated, the right to marry, and so on. *But we Chinese consider these rights to be dangerous* . . . . Freedom by decree is not fit to be called democracy, for unlike Western democracy, it fails to provide the most basic human rights.

In democratic nations, democracy flows from the individual and the government has responsibilities towards him . . . . The situation in China is quite different; we praise our government whenever it finally gets around to doing something for us, when in fact the government has done nothing more than fulfil its obligation.

People of other societies believe that criminal accusations arising from casual suspicions harm human dignity. In China, on the other hand, it is not only normal for me to inform on you if I suspect you of something, but a positive virtue as well . . . . Democracy will never take root in a society like ours . . . .

In December 1986, a local election of the people's representative at UST triggered a student demonstration, and 10,000 UST students marched to the provincial party headquarters to ask for a more democratic system to nominate candidates for the National People's Congress (candidates were nominated by the party). Students in more than 150 universities and colleges joined the 'struggle', and demonstrations were held in most of the big cities across the country; Beijing students marched to Tiananmen Square and held their slogan-shouting, flag-waving demonstrations there. Though the unrest was sparked more by the crisis created by urban reforms (inflation and recession) than by any real demand for democracy (the concept was not fully understood by the students), the Conservatives capitalized on the students' admiration for Western political institutions and their naïve outbursts against the party and its ideology. Slogans such as 'Marxism, Leninism, Thought of Mao Zedong, Go to Hell' helped the Conservatives to exaggerate the danger posed to the party and the state and provided them with an opportunity to exert pressure on Deng Xiaoping to suppress the agitation.

The party's response to the demonstrations was double-edged. On the one hand, it made what appeared to be a major concession by declaring that in the future anybody who was nominated by ten citizens could stand for elections. On the other, a new rule made it obligatory for organizers of demonstrations to first register with the police. The citizen's nomination concession, in reality, was quite meaningless because the nominated candidate had to be approved by an 'election committee' before his name could appear on the ballot list.

Student activities petered out by February 1987, but the damage had been done. The left had made a comeback, and Deng had yielded to Conservative pressure. Speaking to some of the high cadres of the CCP, Deng said:

> The recent student unrest is not going to lead to any major disturbances. But because of its nature it must be taken seriously. Firm measures must be taken against any student who creates trouble at Tiananmen Square. The rules and regulations on marches and demonstrations . . . . have the force of law and should be resolutely enforced. No concessions should be made in this matter . . . .
>
> When disturbance breaks out in a place, it's because the leaders there didn't take a firm, clear-cut stand . . . .
>
> I have read Fang Lizhi's speeches. He doesn't sound like a Communist Party member at all. Why do we keep people like him in the party? *He should be expelled, not just persuaded to quit* . . . . . .
>
> *Without leadership of the Communist Party and without socialism, there is no future for China.*
>
> Bourgeois liberalization would plunge the country into turmoil once more. Bourgeois liberalization means rejection of the party's

leadership; there would be nothing to unite our one billion people, and the party would itself lose all power to fight . . . . .

(In fighting bourgeois liberalization) we should not be afraid that it will damage our reputation abroad.

In his speech, Deng also asserted that the party could not 'do without dictatorship', and ominously warned that if 'some people provoke bloodshed' the party would use its dictatorial powers. Is it really so surprising then that Deng brought out the tanks eighteen months later to put down the student movement?

In January 1987, not only were Fang Lizhi and Liu Binyan expelled from the party, but Hu Yaobang was removed from the general secretaryship of the party for being 'soft and lax in the face of bourgeois liberalization'. Although the unceremonious sacking of the party chief, the man chosen by Deng as his successor, may have hurt Deng's prestige to a certain degree, Deng had sacrificed Hu not only to appease the Conservatives but because Deng genuinely wanted to rectify the swing to the right. But at the same time, since Deng had no desire to see his reform programmes demolished, he promptly replaced Hu Yaobang with his other protégé, the Reformer, Zhao Ziyang.

Zhao Ziyang, in his new post of acting party general secretary, faced a practically impossible task: he had to placate leftist demands without giving up reform policies. The Conservatives, exploiting Deng's recent pronouncements and the campaign against Hu Yaobang, quickly procured the dismissal of some of the Reformers whose loyalty to Hu was well known; they were replaced with leftists. They then extended their influence over the press, disciplined reporters who had supported liberal policies and cracked down on 'liberal' writers. The Conservatives went so far as to revive the 'Learn from Lei Feng' campaign and put Deng in a quandary by hailing him as the person who had upheld the 'Lei Feng's spiritual values' since 1978.

In the economic field, the Conservatives, ostensibly to counter 'wholesale Westernization', made some headway in re-asserting the Maoist model of centralized controls and centralized planning. Ironically, this reactivation of Maoism and the scramble for power by the leftists boded ill for the Conservatives because Deng could not countenance politics going so far to the left.

By mid-year, Deng came to the defence of the beleaguered Zhao Ziyang and dismissed a few of the most powerful Conservative leaders from their posts. More importantly, by some arm-twisting and political manoeuvering, Deng persuaded the veteran party leaders to retire from their official positions and move to the Central Advisory Commission. He thus removed them from direct participation in day-to-day politics (four key Conservative leaders were among the ten who retired from the Politburo). To help the Conservatives save face, Deng also stepped down from all but one of the top leadership positions he held, retaining only the chairmanship of the Military Affairs Commission.

Made in the interest of 'rejuvenating the party', these changes were confirmed at the thirteenth Party Congress, which met in October/November 1987. Deng's desire to see younger and more educated persons emerge as the 'third echelon' of the party leadership was also fulfilled, and this was reflected in the altered composition of the Central Committee elected at the thirteenth Congress: 150 of the 348 members of the last Central Committee, many of the veterans of long standing, had been replaced by new faces; and seventy-three per cent of new Central Committee, twice as many as before, held college degrees. The average age of the members of the Standing Committee of the Politburo, the very top of the party pyramid, dropped by nearly eleven years from that of the previous body.

Deng Xiaoping, however, still had not eradicated all leftist influence. Though the Reformers did maintain a majority in the Politburo, there was a rough parity between the left and the right in the Standing Committee of the Politburo, with the balance tilting slightly in favour of the right. So, while the congress confirmed Zhao Ziyang's appointment as general secretary, it also elevated Li Ping, a Moderate Reformer, to the Politburo Standing Committee and to the post of premier. Li Peng's rise obviously was one of the compromises made, because Li was known to side with the Conservatives on the question of the speed at which the reforms should be carried out and the direction they were to take.

(Li was born in Sichuan in 1928, months after his father, a communist party member, had been killed in a battle with the Guomindang forces. It is said that Zhou Enlai 'adopted' the boy and looked after his upbringing and education. Li was already a party member when, at the age of twenty, he was sent to the Soviet Union to study electrical engineering in 1948. He returned home in 1955. In 1966, he was appointed director of the Beijing Electricity Power Administration. Appointed as vice-minister in the central cabinet in 1979, Li rose to be vice-premier in 1983, a member of the Politburo and a full minister in charge of education in 1985, and premier in 1987.)

Since all the compromises had been worked out before the meeting of the party congress, the congress itself displayed a facade of unity and unanimously confirmed Deng's reform policies. One of the most important contributions made by congress to post-Mao China was its ratification of a redefined ideology. Deng had been working without a developmental model and without a theory to guide his modernization programs. At last, the country was given a 'scientific' framework for growth and change. A novel ideological justification of capitalistic reform policies was presented to the congress by Zhao in his state-of-the-party address. Zhao's thesis was startlingly simple but bold: China was still at the 'primary stage of socialism'. With this pronouncement, Zhao tried to undo all Maoist thinking that had been associated with the communes, egalitarianism and revolutionary upheavals.

Zhao lauded the party's achievement in having overthrown 'the reactionary rule of imperialism, feudalism and bureaucratic-capitalism'. He then added that 'Precisely because our socialism has emerged from the womb of a semi-colonial, semi-feudal society, with the productive forces lagging far behind those of the developed capitalist countries, we are destined to go through a very long primary stage. During this stage we shall accomplish industrialization and commercialization, socialization and modernization of production, *which many other countries have achieved under capitalistic conditions.*'

Marx's socialism could only come to a highly industrialized society. China would become such a society in the next hundred or more years by making the 'development of productive forces' its 'major goal', 'the centre of all our work'. According to Zhao, 'Helping to expand the productive forces should become the point of departure in our consideration of all problems, and the basic criterion in judging all our work.' Therefore, China must keep reforming, adhere to the Open Door policy, develop a commodity economy and let public ownership play a dominant role, and 'encourage some people to become rich first'.

Zhao also referred to the need for political restructuring; he mentioned separating party and state functions, streamlining government organs, establishing a public service system to recruit officials through an examination system, making elections more democratic, and strengthening the legal framework and the role of the legislative body (the National People's Congress). Very adroitly, he separated the issues of political reform and economic modernization by confining the issue of bourgeois liberalization to the 'political/ideological sphere' *within* the party.

However, and here is the rub, all the economic and political tasks had to be carried out 'while adhering to the Four Cardinal Principles'.

The 'reform congress' appeared to be a victory for the Reformers and a personal triumph for Zhao Ziyang. Presumably, Zhao could now move forward resolutely with his plans to open markets, 'not only for consumer goods and raw materials but money (independent banking, stock exchanges), labour, technology (enterprises could buy technology from independent research and development institutes), information (a free press? radio? and TV?) and real estate (the right for enterprises and individuals to buy and sell land, buildings, and houses); to remove price controls; and to throw open more areas to foreign capital and investment.' But this was not to be. Zhao's grand vision was soon to dissolve in the face of China's economic and political reality. In the inner-party debates preceding the congress, the Reformers had conceded that the precipitous pace of the reforms had resulted in massive inflation and that prices needed to be controlled rather than de-controlled. Zhao's report to the congress, at best, had presented a long-term view of reform. It had neither dealt with the economic ills facing the country, nor provided any specific course of action to be followed in the immediate future. However, since the political climate after the congress had swung to the right, Zhao tried to press forward with the reform programmes in 1988, declaring that 'the pace of reforms is not fast enough'.

Zhao, who himself had a limited education, was guided by a 'think tank' composed of young economists and political scientists, who contributed many far-fetched ideas and theories in a typical ivory tower fashion. The notion, which was touted widely, that 'socialism should imbibe all the positive fruits developed by capitalism' led to some bizarre strategies. For example, Zhao revealed a master plan, according to which large coastal areas (with a total population of 200,000,000) were to be converted into Special Economic Zones where Western-style marketing could be carried on, and it was proposed that the island of Hainan (which was given the status of a full-fledged province) be fully opened to international marketing practices and be turned into another Hong Kong. Even Deng, in one of his euphoric moods, had called for the establishment of 'a few Hong Kongs' on the mainland. The rationale was that the coastal zone, which already had experience in international marketing practices, should be allowed to 'develop and get rich first, and then bring prosperity to the hinterland'. This approach was based on the same 'trickle-down' notion that had been manifested in the 'let some people get rich first' policies.

Zhao, backed by Deng, also set the stage for dissolving the controlled pricing system in three to five years. The Reformers hoped that the inflation that was bound to accompany the de-controlling of prices would be absorbed by linking wages to price increases through an indexing system. Some held that 'progress' was being made.

By mid-year the value of industrial production rose seventeen per cent over 1987, but productivity remained low, and many factories were operating at only fifty per cent to seventy per cent of capacity. Deficit financing and a soaring foreign debt appeared to be getting out of control. Inflation, officially calculated at fifteen per cent, had actually jumped to thirty per cent. News of imminent price de-controls led to hoarding, panic buying, and massive corruption; similarly, rumours of currency devaluation resulted in runs on banks.

In the meantime, the opening of the country to private and collectively owned 'capitalist' enterprises, had lured individuals and institutions (the PLA included), to set up undertakings, ranging from roadside stalls to factories and hotels. In June 1988, these activities were given legal status with the introduction of the Temporary Statute on Private Enterprises, which also permitted businesses to be bought and sold or inherited.

Though most of the several tens of millions of individuals engaged in private business were persons who otherwise would have been unemployed and who were small-scale entrepreneurs (tailors, hairdressers, vendors of food, etc.), many others were moonlighting to supplement their inadequate fixed incomes. Among the latter were the ill-paid school and college teachers, whose earnings from one day of moonlighting often equalled their entire month's salary. By mid-year, eighteen million professional technical personnel (thirteen per cent of the national pool) were holding some kind of a second job.

High party cadres also got into the act by becoming 'consultants' to firms that were doing business with the cadres' bureaucratic organizations. This was theoretically an illegal activity that created a conflict of interest, but in the money-crazed environment nobody paid attention to rules and regulations. These corrupt and venal, wheeling-dealing cadres soon built up huge private fortunes.

However, the real profiteers were located in the 400,000 business companies that had sprung up by 1988; sixty-four per cent of these were involved in commercial activity and employed nearly 41,000,000 persons. According to an investigative report published by Beijing in 1989, after the Tiananmen Massacre:

> Private businesses, collective enterprises and state-owned factories were not the only units involved in the nationwide craze for business. Party and government organizations and even the army, public security and judicial departments eagerly entered the distribution field of materials. Abusing their power and taking advantage of the incomplete reform measures, many companies engaged in illegal management activities reaping huge profits by buying and reselling critically short raw materials and common, everyday commodities in high demand. Their activities increased the burden on both producers and consumers, disturbed the nation's economic order, drove up the price index and the rate of inflation, and disrupted the normal reform process.

Cases of illegal dealings, profiteering from goods in short supply, bribery, embezzlement, racketeering, and blackmail ran into millions.

Corruption blossomed as never before.

By the summer of 1988, the two pernicious by-products of the modernization programmes, corruption and inflation, had assumed such menacing proportions that the people began to lose faith in the government's will and ability to solve the problem.

Li Peng, the moderate Reformer, led the opposition and began to subvert Zhao's plans by insisting that further steps to introduce free market operations be carried out gradually, cautiously and in an environment of economic 'stability'. He argued that the reform policies must be geared to the 'acceptance level' of the masses and that the overheated economy and inflation must be brought under control.

In the face of mounting public opposition, the Reformers had to give in. In the fall of 1988, a policy of retrenchment was introduced and the government declared that not only prices of seventy-two major commodities would continue to be controlled, but that price reform in 1989 would be limited. By the end of the year, Deng, too, was persuaded that centralized controls needed to be re-exerted so that an austerity programme could be launched. However, the dislocated economy could not be located by fiat. The money supply continued to grow, inflation continued to spiral, and corruption continued to raise its ugly head. In April 1989, after six months of belt-tightening measures, the economy was worse off than a year earlier: unemployment had risen while the inflation still hovered around thirty per cent. Not surprisingly, there was a nationwide revival of pro-Mao sentiment; according to one report, the slogan 'We'd rather have the stable prices of Chairman Mao than the high prices of Deng Xiaoping,' was heard across the country.*

It was under these conditions that the students began their agitation against the government. The decision of the government to stop guaranteeing jobs to students graduating from high schools made matters worse. The educated youth, the future intelligentsia, no longer had any confidence in either the Reformers or the Moderate Reformers, or for that matter in Deng Xiaoping. Practically a year before the Spring Massacre,

---

* Quoted by Willy Wo-Lap Lam in his most insightful work, *The Era of Zhao Ziyang*, Hong Kong: A.B. Books and Stationary, 1989, p. 252.

in June 1988, students at Beijing University had already put up posters attacking Zhao Ziyang, Li Ping and Deng Xiaoping by name. Instead of trying to placate the students, the leaders tried to frighten them by saying that 'rightist troublemakers' would be severely punished. Broad hints were also dropped that foreigners and the VOA had a hand in fermenting trouble on the campuses. Despite the clamp down, student discontent continued to simmer through 1988 and the early months of 1989.

The leaders recognized that there was an educational crisis in China and that intellectuals needed to be better rewarded for their work. Indeed, Deng Xiaoping had told a visiting delegation in 1988 that, 'our biggest mistake over the past ten years has been insufficient development of education.' It was expected that the National People's Congress would take up the issue of educational reform in its session in March 1989. Unfortunately, the discussion of the party platform was postponed to April.

We will never know what that platform would have brought the students, or whether the students would have continued to wait even longer for ameliorative policies if Hu Yaobang's death on 15 April 1989, had not ended the two years of relative tranquility and led to the large-scale demonstrations that terminated in the Tiananmen Square Massacre.

5

The Tiananmen Square Massacre

Hu Yaobang, ex-general secretary of the Chinese Communist Party, died of a heart attack on 15 April 1989.

On the following morning, which happened to be a Sunday, 300 college students (Beijing has sixty colleges and universities with a student population of about 150,000) made their way to Tiananmen Square to pay homage to the memory of Hu Yaobang. Who could have foretold that from these small beginnings a storm was to rise in the otherwise placid city of Beijing and force an unpopular leadership to use guns against its citizens?

In reviewing the events of the Spring Revolt, one is struck by the spontaneity of the student 'democracy movement', which initially lacked both organization and leadership and till the very end never developed a definite programme of political action.

The students' march to Tiananmen Square to lay a wreath in Hu's memory at the foot of the Monument of the People's Heroes could not be considered a 'demonstration' in the strict sense of the term—demonstrations were prohibited under the law except when officially permitted—it was more an expression of mourning which the leaders could not deny.

Having realized that Hu's death gave them an opportunity to vent their dissatisfaction with the authorities, the number of student 'mourners' (demonstrators in fact) increased every day from 16 April on; it finally reached a figure of several tens of thousands on the day of Hu's funeral (22 April). Organized according to their institutions, many of these students brought along banners extolling democracy and decrying dictatorship. Earlier, on 19 April, some of the more daring ones went to Zhongnanhai, where the principal Chinese leaders reside, shouting slogans and demanding that the leaders come out to talk to them. The police broke up this rally; though none of the protesters was arrested, some students were beaten in the process. The authorities, worried by the escalation of the demonstrations, made repeated declarations that they would not allow any group to defy the constitutional ban on public protests and that the 'small number' of troublemakers who were inciting the students would be 'severely dealt with'. However, neither the Beijing authorities nor the central government did anything to carry out these threats.

There were many reasons for student discontent, most of them traceable to Deng's new political and economic policies. The students resented the political system that appeared to be built on a vast network of massive corruption which allowed a few to exploit the many. While they themselves lived six or eight to a room and after graduation were arbitrarily assigned jobs in undesirable locations on salaries that were often lower than the wages of many uneducated workers, they saw officials and wealthy private entrepreneurs thriving on nepotism, bribes, and kickbacks. Many bureaucrats and businessmen lived lavishly, went about in foreign cars and had the means to send their children abroad for education. The thirty per cent inflation rate, also a consequence of the new economic policies, had further undermined the already meagre living standards of the students and their poorly paid teachers. Also, the students deeply resented the controls on the freedom of expression which kept them from airing their grievances.

On 22 April, after the funeral ceremonies in the Great Hall of the People, which stands on one side of Tiananmen Square and where all the leaders of the party and government had gathered, three students, who had by then emerged as 'leaders', tried to present a petition addressed to premier Li Peng. In the manner of petitioners in Imperial China, the three kneeled on the steps outside the Great Hall of the People; one held the scroll listing student demands above his head. The symbolism was not lost on the crowd: the dictators of today, like the emperors of yesterday, could not be approached by democratic means.

The petition called for Hu Yaobang's rehabilitation, publication of the personal assets of the leaders and their family members, price controls on consumer goods, lifting of restrictions on publications, and a 'dialogue' with Li Peng. No official stepped forth to receive the petition.

HU YAOBANG'S LIFE: A RECAPITULATION

Hu was born in Mao Zedong's home province of Hunan in 1915. He joined the Communist Youth League of China at the age of fifteen and became a full party member at eighteen. After a life of dedication to party work, Hu rose through the ranks to reach the highest echelons of party leadership. In 1980, Deng Xiaoping designated Hu as his heir-apparent by getting him appointed general secretary of the party; Hu was also duly elected to the Standing Committee of the Politburo.

In 1981, Hu Yaobang presented the Party Central Committee a re-evaluation of party history, which no doubt had received the approval of Deng. In his speech, Hu openly attacked Mao Zedong for his mistakes and shortcomings. 'Mao Zedong,' said Hu, 'became overconfident and more and more divorced from reality and the masses and, in particular, from the party's collective leadership, and often rejected and even suppressed correct opinions that differed from his.' This report marked the demise of ultra-leftist Maoist ideology and gave promise of relatively greater freedom of thought. Hu, eager to modernize China, was even more enthusiastic than Deng in overturning Maoist economic policies and introducing the new reform programmes. As a part of the 'Open Door' policy that sought, and welcomed, an inflow of Western technology, science, and capital into China, Hu also adopted some ideas of political liberalization, which unfortunately, were denounced by Deng as being inimical to political stability.

Then, in 1986, a student movement calling for 'more democracy' was ill-received by Deng, who declared that 'bourgeois liberalism' was leading the country to capitalism and undermining socialism and that the movement needed to be crushed. As general secretary, it was Hu's duty to impose ideological controls on the intellectuals and keep the 'bourgeois liberalization' tendency from spreading. Since he had shown a lenient attitude towards the intellectuals, he was held accountable for not cracking down on the students and dismissed from his post in 1987. At that time Deng commented:

> Over the past few years, efforts to counter the bourgeois liberalization tendency have been insufficient. I have repeatedly emphasized the problem. However, our party has failed to take effective measures in this respect. This is an important mistake of Comrade Hu Yaobang . . . . Our decision about his dismissal is fair and reasonable.

There were other grounds for his dismissal, too, but for this particular reason Hu gained the respect of the students and the intellectuals.

Hu spent the last two years of his life in relative oblivion.

If the students had been met by a senior official and the petition accepted, it might have marked the end of the so-called demonstrations. The government and the party may have been technically correct in not accepting the petition from some self-appointed student leaders, who had not followed the correct procedures for representing their complaints, but this was an extraordinary situation which called for some flexibility. Such flexibility may have been forthcoming if the party leaders had not been involved in an inner party struggle for power, with (as we shall see later) one side trying to use the student demonstrations to its advantage. As things turned out, the student leaders, humiliated and insulted, called for a continued boycott of classes and further demonstrations through 4 May, the day on which the nation was to mark the seventieth anniversary of the 4 May Incident.

Signs of a Hard Line

After Hu Yaobang's funeral, the students' decision to carry on the demonstrations made their activities truly illegal and took on the characteristics of a direct confrontation with authority. Earlier, in 1980, the National People's Congress, under the guidance of Deng Xiaoping, had adopted a special resolution to delete an article of the constitution that gave the citizens the right to 'speak out freely, air their views fully, hold great debates and write big character posters'. Deng had defended this decision, arguing that only those who 'worship Western "democracy" are always insisting on these rights'. And it was Hu Yaobang's inability to repress the student movement in 1986 that brought on his dismissal. Now, three years later, the students by demonstrating for demonstration's sake and speaking out freely were insisting on regaining exactly this right.

Constitutional legality notwithstanding, the leaders were not united on the question of how the student demonstrations were to be handled. The Standing Committee of the Politburo was split between those who favoured a soft line advocated by Zhao Ziyang (who had replaced Hu as party general secretary and shared many of Hu's modernization ideals), and those who believed with Deng and premier Li Peng that disorder would lead to anarchy unless the demonstrators were suppressed with a firm hand. In the absence of Zhao, who had left for Korea on an official trip immediately following the funeral, Deng is reported to have told a meeting of the Politburo that a hard line was called for and that, 'We should not be afraid of bloodshed or pressure from international public opinion.' He suggested that troops should be used if necessary.

Deng's position was reflected in an editorial of the *People's Daily* on 26 April, perhaps written by Deng himself, which labelled the demonstrations an '*organized conspiracy* to sow chaos . . . . poison the people's minds, create national turmoil and sabotage the nation's political stability by aiming to *overthrow the party leaders and the socialist system.*' From his point of view, Deng was not far wrong: demonstrations, though small in comparison to those in Beijing, had spread to half-a-dozen other cities of China, including Shanghai, and indirect attacks on Deng, indicated by small, smashed bottles left on the pavements (in spoken parlance 'Xiaoping' can mean 'small bottle'), were rapidly being replaced by explicit demands for Deng to surrender his position of power.

The Line Softens

The Beijing students' response to the editorial and the orders prohibiting public gatherings was to escalate the demonstrations. Stung by what they considered to be false accusations, over a 100,000 students (150,000 according to some estimates), many more thousands than had turned out in any of the earlier parades, marched to Tiananmen Square on 27 April.

The popular support from cheering bystanders, and the lack of will shown by the security police and soldiers to block the student parade, makes one wonder whether the general citizenry had made common cause with the students and whether even some of the leaders were quietly encouraging the demonstrators.

That evening the government announced that it would agree to open a dialogue with the students, but the students must return to the campuses, adopt a 'calm and reasonable' attitude, and allow the official students' association to represent them. Although this was not a major concession, the students felt that the government was weakening. Exhilarated by this apparent 'victory', they rejected the government conditions, particularly the stipulation that they speak through the official students' association, which they regarded as a tool of the party. However, it was patently true that the students themselves had no recognized leaders who could command their common allegiance. The 'democratic' organizing committees in most colleges were large and unwieldy. Beijing University, for example, had a committee of sixty-three members! Perhaps, because of this problem, the uneasy stand-off between the students and the Beijing party and government officials could not be resolved. Some Beijing leaders did disclose their salaries and financial assets before holding meetings with the official students' union, but this did not impress the demonstrating students who continued to boycott classes.

Zhao Ziyang, who evidently had used the student agitation to press for more liberal policies within the party, was now anxious that the students stop the demonstration so that he could show his opponents that they were wrong in their belief that the students were an unruly, uncontrollable mob out to undermine national stability. There was an urgency in Zhao's appeal to the students, on 3 May, when he remarked: 'if stability is destroyed what can be achieved? Can science and democracy be achieved? They cannot. All that will result is turmoil.' Zhao, no doubt, was hoping that the students would restrain their activities on the following day, the historic anniversary of the 4 May Incident, and not mar the dignity of the officially organized events. But the student movement had acquired a life of its own and was a force that could no longer be controlled. The students' reply perhaps was best expressed in a ditty which was sung to the tune of a popular song, 'Follow Your Feeling':

> The country is following the Communist Party,
> The Communist Party is following Zhao Ziyang,
> Zhao Ziyang is following Deng Xiaoping,
> Deng Xiaoping is following his feelings.

As a result, the official functions on 4 May were totally overshadowed by the massive demonstration organized by the students who, joined by many professional groups (journalists being prominent among them) and workers, marched into the city from various directions to 'capture' Tiananmen Square. The workers, risking official reprimand, had combined forces with the students because the workers, too, had grievances stemming from inflation and the rising cost of basic commodities. It is significant that the workers, who outnumbered the students, did not go on strike on their own—they marched along with the students, who formed the nucleus of this mass movement. Similarly, the journalists, offended by the manner in which they had been forced to suppress the news of the demonstrations, came out in support of the movement because the students were calling for greater freedom of the press. The government's proscription of the editions of *Science and Technology Daily* and *World Economic Herald*, which had published accounts of the demonstrations without getting the approval of the censors, and the dismissal of Qin Benli, the editor of the latter publication, had alienated the journalists and inspired the students to publish their own campus newspapers so that the people could learn the 'truth'.

The hard liners were shocked by the unexpectedly high turnout of non-students and angered because the demonstrators, by blithely exploiting the presence of foreign reporters and TV cameramen and freely expressing their opinions for international viewers, were embarrassing the Chinese government. However, the hard liners still made no real attempt to stop or suppress the parades. Perhaps Zhao Ziyang had been able to convince them that calm would return after 4 May. Speaking to the delegates of the Asian Development Bank in the Great Hall of the People on 4 May, Zhao made some remarks that can be construed as conciliatory to the student cause, while at the same time indicating a possible future scenario of government action. After asserting that the students were generally satisfied with the reforms in China and that he was sure that the demonstrations would wind down soon, he added, 'What (the students) are most dissatisfied with are errors and mistakes in the government's work . . . . The student's demands for correcting errors so as to march forward coincide with those of the party and the government.' Obviously, the intent of Zhao's remarks was that he agreed with the student criticism and that the party and government would try and rectify the problems.

The days between 4 May and 13 May were critical. The inner party debate on student unrest appeared to have shifted in the direction of the soft liners. The change in line may have been an attempt to defuse the student movement before the Soviet President, Mikhail Gorbachev, arrived on 15 May for the first Sino–Soviet summit in thirty years. Deng Xiaoping was anxious to make this occasion a memorable one because the normalization of Sino–Soviet relations would have marked the high point of his dynamic and eventful rule. In any event, Li Peng, representing the party hard liners, made promises of continuing 'the dialogue with the students' and confirmed his good intentions by allowing official newspapers to publish fuller accounts of student protests and demands.

Readers were pleasantly surprised on 5 May when newspapers, which had so far studiously provided only limited coverage of the demonstrations, suddenly displayed a new openness, devoting their front pages to photographs of Beijing streets jammed with banner-waving students and reports on demonstrations and riots in Beijing and other cities. Although the objectivity of the reports, which explicitly mentioned student demands, was tinctured by statements that the demonstrations were technically illegal and that the new students' organizations had 'failed to observe legal procedures laid down by the constitution (meaning that they were not officially approved)', the articles nevertheless were refreshing for their overall candidness.

This helped in easing tensions, and many of the student leaders, including the charismatic Wuer Kaixi (a freshman in Beijing Normal University), announced that on 5 May class boycotts would end. However, some students, who had found the outdoor activity more pleasing than sitting in musty classrooms, refused to take any orders from their 'leaders' and continued their demonstrations, though in a desultory fashion.

At this stage the journalists added to the confusion by demanding a dialogue with the leaders. On 9 May 1,000 journalists from official news organizations sent a petition to the government criticizing press censorship on the grounds that limited, or distorted, press coverage of the student demonstrations had 'attracted criticism at home and abroad'. The action of the journalists was hailed by the students and provided them a new opportunity to revive their flagging movement. Perhaps because they were tired of walking miles from the campus to Tiananmen Square, or perhaps because they wanted to add a new eye-catching, news-worthy dimension to their activity, the small number of students still demonstrating had begun to parade on bicycles. On 10 May, they held a giant 'bicycle parade' and 10,000 bicyclists rode to the gates of Radio Beijing, China Central Television, Xinhua (New China) News Agency, and the *People's Daily* in support of the journalists. At each stop they shouted slogans such as: '*People's Daily* you lie to the people', 'Central TV you turn white into black'. Although, even this parade was smaller than earlier ones (not only in size but also in school representation—only sixteen institutions were represented), it did help to maintain pressure on the government.

In preparing for Gorbachev's visit, plans had been made for Gorbachev's motorcade to travel via Changan Avenue to Tiananmen Square where a welcoming ceremony was to take place. Later Gorbachev was to be guest of honour at a formal banquet in the Great Hall of the People that flanks Tiananmen Square, and a ceremony had been planned for him to lay a wreath at the Monument of the People's Heroes that stands in the Square. He was also scheduled to visit the imperial palace complex in the Forbidden City. The leaders were particularly anxious that there be no demonstrators or any sign of disturbance in Tiananmen Square or along the Changan Avenue (the east-west road that runs between the square and the Forbidden City). On 12 May, a government spokesman met with the students and requested them not to demonstrate during the Chinese–

Soviet summit meeting on the 15th.

The students' response was totally unanticipated. On the 13th, two days before Gorbachev's arrival, 1,000 students, supported by 15,000 of their colleagues, occupied a section of Tiananmen Square and began a hunger strike to press their demand for talks. They rejected the government's overture that officials would meet twenty of their representatives on the 15th and allow the press to publish a partial report of the talks; the students felt that the figure of twenty was too small and that 'partial' reporting was unacceptable. The students also spurned Zhao Ziyang's plea that 'it is unreasonable for students or other citizens . . . to obstruct international talks or the Sino–Soviet summit'. To add insult to injury, the students requested the Soviet embassy to arrange a meeting between them and Gorbachev. (The Soviet embassy's diplomatic reply was that such a meeting could not be arranged because of Gorbachev's schedule.) On the 14th, the number of hunger-striking students had risen to 2,000 (later, it would reach the figure of 3,000).

The basic demands of the students were still rather simple: government officials should hold direct talks with them and televise the entire proceedings; the government should retract the derogatory 26 April editorial; the government should publish a favourable re-evaluation of the student movement and recognize the independent student union. A high level party delegation met with the students repeatedly on the 14th, the eve of Gorbachev's arrival, but was unable to coax the youth to leave the Square. Several official deadlines for clearing the plaza passed without drawing any positive response from the protesters. The students, who had put up portraits of Gorbachev and banners with slogans in Russian, said they would hold their own reception for the great Soviet leader.

The consequence of the student action was a personal humiliation for Deng Xiaoping: plans for the imposing reception at Tiananmen Square were cancelled and Gorbachev was received at the airport; Gorbachev had to be brought to the ceremony in the Great Hall of the People through the rear door; and Gorbachev had to cancel his visit to the Forbidden City. What a loss of face for Deng! Also, the attention of the international press corps of some 1,200 journalists shifted from the summit to the students. Deng lost his moment of glory.

The Revolt: Phase One

The period from 13 May to 4 June, can be divided into two phases. In the first phase, which lasted seven days from the 13th to the 19th, Zhao Ziyang appears to have made his last ineffectual effort to win his case while the hard liners prepared to take more drastic action.

There was great popular sympathy for the innocent, courageous, youthful hunger strikers. Beijingers not only came out in large numbers to watch the students in their tent city (not an unexpected development), but offered them food and drink and monetary support. Many Beijingers, from street vendors and unemployed youth to hotel employees, nurses, airline employees, policemen, and teachers, professors, lawyers, journalists and other professionals, joined the demonstrators and paraded in the Square flaunting their own banners. The common theme of their protest was that the government did not listen to the people. While the officials and party leaders, inside the Great Hall of the People, made speeches at the banquet for Gorbachev, the crowds shouted anti-government slogans on the outside. Then, on the 17th, the day Gorbachev was to leave Beijing, an estimated 1,000,000 citizens of the capital gathered at the Square.

By this time, the Beijing government had lost control of some of the vital parts of the city where the 'rebels' had set up their own mini-government. The students' policing units directed traffic and kept 'life-line roads' open for ambulances; their medical dispensaries looked after the sick; their print shops produced propaganda pamphlets and leaflets (as well as T-shirts with provocative slogans); and their accounting office maintained records of monies and other commodities received as gifts. The 'rebels' also commandeered buses and organized a unit of motorcyclists, who dashed at high speed through the city carrying messages and news. They were helped in their endeavours by thousands of volunteers.

Reporters from foreign TV networks, who had come to cover the summit, stayed on to cover what they considered to be 'the most exciting development in post-Mao China'. The students were not oblivious to their newsworthiness. They began to put up placards printed in English with slogans like 'Give Me Democracy Or Give Me Death' and 'Hello, Mr Democracy'. They also had a host of interpreters ready for any reporter who wanted an interview or the translation of slogans in Chinese which were getting increasingly provocative (such as, 'Hang Li Peng', and 'Down with Deng Xiaoping'). The students willingly stopped in the middle of a parade to give the foreign TV cameramen a 'good' shot.

The hunger strikers remained the main attraction and provided the focus of the protest movement. Their every move was duly caught by the ever-watchful eyes of the TV cameras. Audiences abroad were impressed by the immense outpouring of popular support for the hunger strikers and, unconsciously, began to sympathize with the critics of the government.

On the 18th, in what appeared to be a gesture of reconciliation or 'capitulation', the government conceded to one of the major demands of the students and decided to let Li Peng hold a nationally-televised meeting with student representatives, something that would have been unthinkable just a week earlier. Here was high drama at its best. The viewers saw a bunch of casually (some may even say 'shabbily') dressed students, some of them, like Wuer Kaixi, still on hunger strike, with tubes sticking out of their nostrils, facing a dignified and severe-looking premier Li Peng, who hardly had time to sit down, was rebuked by Wuer Kaixi (who later fainted from hunger and exhaustion) for arriving late. This was an unprecedented public humiliation of a high official. Student leader Wang Dan also spoke sternly to Li Peng and demanded that he stop evading the issues.

Li, obviously angered, replied sharply:

> In the last few days, Beijing has fallen into a kind of anarchy. I hope you will think it over. What will result from the situation? China's government is responsible for the whole people. We will not sit idly by doing nothing. We have to safeguard the people's property and our students' lives. We have to safeguard our factories. *We have to defend our socialist system.* (and he warned) 'The situation will not develop as you wish and expect even though you have patriotic zeal . . . . *I hope you will deeply consider what the final consequences will be if the situation deteriorates.*'

Li had made it clear that force would be used to quell the protests if the 'turmoil' continued.

The students, who had been so anxious to open a dialogue, now felt that a dialogue was not enough. They wanted the removal of the country's senior leaders, and a fresh banner raised outside one of the colleges read: 'Dump the Politburo.'

The party hard liners had also made their last move. They hoped they had succeeded in showing the world that the students, however patriotic and well-intentioned, were naïve and that there was an unseen hand pushing them in the direction of confrontation. Those who thought that the hard liners had given in because they were afraid the student hunger strike would galvanize the nation against the party, were quite mistaken. It appears that in biding their time and letting the students get out of hand, the hard liners were setting the stage for a sterner and stronger response.

On the 19th morning, Li Peng and Zhao Ziyang went to the Square to visit the hunger-striking students. Li's visit was brief, but Zhao spent a longer time with the students and the cameras caught him talking softly with them with tears in his eyes. Zhao, we can surmise in hindsight, was aware that he had lost his cause and the policy debate had finally been resolved in favour of a hard line. The gist of what he told the students is as follows:

> I am sorry we have come too late. Your criticism of us is justified. I am here to ask your forgiveness. I am just saying your bodies have become very weak. Your hunger strike is already in its seventh day . . . . You have good intentions. You want our country to be better. The problems you raised will eventually be resolved. But things are complicated, and there must be a process to resolve these problems.

He called on the students to end the fast adding that he was 'too old' but that they were 'still young and will live to see the modernization of China'. This was Zhao's last public appearance. In a few days he would be officially dismissed from all his posts. Did Zhao have foreknowledge of this when he rather indiscreetly told Gorbachev that the Central Committee had adopted a (hitherto undisclosed) resolution in 1987 that Deng would be consulted on all important matters? Was he putting all the blame for the troubles on Deng? Or was he making Deng out to be the new Mao whose despotism had caused the trouble?

At 9 p.m. on the 19th the students seriously considered calling off the hunger strike, but on learning about the party's secret decision to declare martial law and move troops into Beijing (the information was leaked to them by some party 'high up'), they changed their mind and decided to stand firm. Wuer Kaixi made a heroic statement: 'We are fighting for the prosperity of our motherland and the glory of China. We will fight to the end.'

The Revolt: Phase Two

It was significant that when Li Peng gave the televised speech late in the night of the 19th–20th in which he analyzed the state of the nation and declared martial law, Zhao Ziyang was not among the Politburo members who stood behind Li. Many weeks later the world would learn that Zhao had refused to go along with the hard line decision and had taken 'sick leave'.

Li spoke of the handful of evil-doers who were holding the hunger-strikers 'hostage' and creating 'anarchy' to 'coerce and force the party and the government to yield to their political demand . . . (which was) to overthrow the leadership of the Communist Party of China'; and that they were doing this by '*concentrating their attack on Comrade Deng Xiaoping*, who has made a great contribution to China's opening to the outside world'. Li stated that he had been told by the student leaders that they could no longer control the situation in Tiananmen Square which had resulted in 'chaos'. He added that '*the situation in Beijing is still worsening and has already affected many other cities in the country.*' For this reason martial law was being declared and the military brought in.

The post-midnight speech of Li Peng was supposed to coincide with the pre-planned, unannounced entrance of 20,000 troops into Beijing. But the government had lost the element of surprise, and the forewarned students and their sympathizers had set up barricades at various entrance points of the city and managed to hold back the People's Liberation Army trucks from entering Beijing. The throngs surrounding the trucks chanted,

SOME EXCERPTS FROM LI'S SPEECH

There have been many incidents in which people broke into local party and government organs, along with beating, smashing, looting, burnings and other undermining activities that seriously violated the law . . . ; this will lead to nationwide turmoil if no quick action is taken to stabilize the situation . . .

Reforms . . . and the fate and the future of the People's Republic are facing serious threat . . . The party and government have pointed out time and again that the students are kind-hearted, and they do not want to create turmoil. Instead, these *patriotic students hope to promote democracy and overcome corruption, and this in line with the goals the party and government have strived to achieve.*

(A handful of conspirators hope to) overthrow the people's government elected by the National People's Congress and totally negate the people's democratic dictatorship. They stir up trouble everywhere, establish secret ties, set up illegal organizations . . . . (They have taken) tolerance as weakness on the part of the party and government. They continue to cook up stories to confuse and poison the masses . . . .

I urgently appeal on behalf of the Party Central Committee and the state council (i.e., on behalf of the party and government):

> To those students now on hunger strike . . .to end the fasting immediately, leave the Square, receive medical treatment and recover their health as soon as possible.
>
> To students and people in all walks of life to immediately stop all demonstrations, and give no more so-called 'support' to the fasting students . . . ; further 'support' will push the fasting students to desperation . . . .
>
> (We) also hope that the people in the capital will fully support the People's Liberation Army, police and armed police in their efforts to maintain order in the capital.

'The people love the People's Army', and 'The People's Army protects the people'. There were also those who jeered at the soldiers and taunted them for trying to crush the common people of China.

The government-controlled loudspeakers in Tiananmen Square repeatedly broadcast Li Peng's speech during the night, but the protesters, instead of dispersing as advised, responded by calling Li Peng and Deng Xiaoping 'fascists' and 'Nazis', and by hoisting banners that demanded their immediate resignation. When martial law was officially imposed at 10 a.m. on 20 May, no troops had reached Tiananmen Square. The demonstrators in the Square were elated and exhilarated by their apparent victory; they felt that there was nothing that could stand in the path of their 'revolution'. Never had the Chinese communist government brought in the army to suppress the common people. Never had the common people challenged the communist authorities in so blatant a manner.

The impasse heightened the crisis within the party. Since the expectation that the declaration of martial law and the bringing in of troops would disperse the citizenry had not been fulfilled, the leaders now were compelled to find a consensus on how far they could go in using violent means to suppress the 'revolt'. Meanwhile, the emboldened students were burning effigies of Li Peng in Nazi uniform (one graffito read: 'Strangle the dictator Li Peng') and plastering the walls with cartoons of Deng Xiaoping whose brain, the slogans said, was 'addled'. Popular support for the deposed Zhao Ziyang made the situation even more intolerable. But a consensus was hard to reach. There were some in the party and the army who sided with Zhao Ziyang, and there were many more who could not accept the idea that guns should be used in any crackdown.

Deng's stand had been clearly stated in the 26 April editorial, but before he could put down the movement by using state violence he needed to eliminate his opposition within the party as well as gain the support of most, if not all, of the army commanders. He had not been seen in public after the Sino–Soviet summit, and there were rumours that he had died. Actually, he was very much alive; he was in the south winning over the regional army commanders.

In Beijing, supporters of Zhao Ziyang tried to persuade the Standing

Committee of the National People's Congress (NPC) to hold an emergency meeting because the constitution was being 'wantonly trampled by a few people'. Two research fellows from the institutes of politics and history under the Chinese Academy of Social Sciences, known for their friendship with Zhao Ziyang, published an article in a Hong Kong paper suggesting that a democratic and legal solution to the student movement would come if 'every member of the NPC Standing Committee and every member of the NPC cast a sacred vote to abolish martial law and dismiss Li Peng as premier'.

Apart from demoralizing the troops, the secret inner party struggle for power had a very disheartening effect on the cadres of the local party and government. From the 20th of May to the 25th, when Li Peng's reappearance on television (after a lapse of six days) dramatized the consolidation of the hard line, people were confused by the contradictory policies being followed by various institutions of the government. Martial law had been declared but not enforced. Why? Lack of information also led to a flood of rumours, all of them unfavourable to the government: Deng Xiaoping was going to retire in America where he would live off the ill-gotten wealth he had deposited in secret bank accounts; Deng had said that it was worth killing 200,000 students to bring twenty years of stability to China; the army commanders had refused to order their troops into Beijing; there was trouble between troops loyal to Deng and those against him; and so on.

How was a Beijinger, or a foreign reader for that matter, supposed to react to reports, excerpted below from an official magazine that covered the period up to late May?

> EXCERPT 1: There is no denying that problems (concerning the freedom of the press) still abound. First of all, most journalists probably agree that a more reasonable system of leadership has to be worked out . . . Undoubtedly, the propagation of party and government policies and views and the dissemination of socialist education among the people remains one of the major functions of the Chinese media. *But it is equally and sometimes even more important for them to voice the peoples' opinions and desires. This*

is particularly true when the party and the government are committing mistakes or stupidities.

EXCERPT 2: *Slogans On the Square*

'To lose the people is to lose all'

That slogan chanted by a group of Beijing University faculty was just one of the many catchy lines that echoed across Beijing's Tiananmen Square last week . . . .

Scholars from the Communications Research Institute chanted, 'We want freedom more than bread.' Next to them stood the editors from the Writers' Publishing House saying, 'Media is the voice of the people, not of any individual.' . . . Not to be left out was the China Youth Political Institute. Their banner proclaimed, 'Democracy and Law are guarantees for social stability. Dictatorship and corruption are the roots of social turbulence.'

Finally, the multitudes of Beijing citizens looking over the waving sea of humanity saw students from the Central Nationalities Institute waving their banner high up in China's brisk spring air (on which was written) '56 Nationalities Call for Democracy'.

EXCERPT 3: On the evening of 19th May more than 100 military vehicles, each packed with over thirty soldiers, were blocked by thousands of Beijing residents . . . seven kilometres from Tiananmen Square, the centre of the capital, where more than 100,000 students are continuing their one-month long demonstrations.

A sixty-year-old woman sat in front of a military car, (and) asked tearfully to (*sic*) the men in the People's Liberation Army uniform not to advance to the Square. 'Those kids (students) are very, very weak, how can you have the heart to suppress them. Beijing supports them. If you insist on moving forward, I would rather your cars roll over my body,' the woman said.

EXCERPT 4: Most people interviewed by *Beijing Review* reporters think the action (martial law) is neither necessary nor justified. They said that there was no looting, arson or violence committed in the city and that the police and the people can handle things by themselves. It is illogical, they said, to send so many troops to cope with the few minor incidents. It's like 'using a cannon to shoot a mosquito', one of them added.

This new spirit of boldness in newspaper reporting continued to find expression even after the declaration of martial law. A contingent of journalists from the *People's Daily* marched to the square on the 22nd with a banner that read, 'Lift Martial Law and Protect the Capital'. The government's vacillation over press control also affected foreign TV networks: the networks were denied the right to transmit their news on 20 May, the ban was lifted on the 22nd and reimposed on the 24th. The foreign networks, however, continued to provide coverage of the Square by flying their newsreels to Hong Kong or Tokyo from where they were duly transmitted to audiences back home.

While the power struggle continued behind the walled compound of Zhongnanhai, Beijing was crippled by food shortages and disruption of vital services. This was largely the result of the military having blocked the key roads that connected Beijing with the rest of the country and which were the communication and distribution arteries of the capital. The students, too, had contributed their bit to the confusion by commandeering 300 buses; 200 were used as roadblocks, others as shelters in the Square. However, Beijing continued to function, though hardly as the 'capital' of China. The visits of some foreign dignitaries, including the Queen of the Netherlands were cancelled, because Beijing could not handle state guests.

It is worth mentioning, once again, that the students' 'mini-government' did a remarkably effective job of helping to run the city under their control. It is also worthy of mention that in spite of the fact that life in the city was becoming more difficult, popular support for the students did not diminish and Beijingers continued to shower the youth with food, clothing and money. Monetary support also poured in from compatriots in Hong Kong, the United States and other Western countries—even from Taiwan. This, of course, only increased the government's suspicion of the 'foreign hand' in the 'conspiracy'. Nevertheless, the 'tent city' in the Square was getting filthy and many students had not had a bath for days.

Foreign reporters and television cameras persisted in extolling the 'revolution' and interviewing the 'revolutionary leaders', though by this time perceptive observers of the Chinese scene had come to discern the complexity of the crisis; they realized that the confrontation was by no stretch of the imagination a revolution and its resolution would come, sooner or later, with the crushing of the protest.

First, it had become evident that the students had no distinguishable ideology. They talked of 'democracy' but had little notion of the term. Lacking the knowledge of democratic practices in other countries, and having had no experience of it in their own, the students used the term 'democracy' as a catchword that implied an opposition to all that they saw as wrong in their communist-party-run government. Within their own organization, they tried to apply democracy by holding meetings and electing committees. In time they had a plethora of committees but no leaders who could command the allegiance of the student body as a whole. Even the recognized leaders repeatedly tried but failed to persuade the students to follow their commands. The *New York Times* reported on 23 May, that splits had developed among student leaders and that 'Wuer Kaixi now seems to be widely criticized after trying twice on (the 22nd) to convince students to leave Tiananmen Square'. The students also held the peculiar notion that democracy meant that the majority must never ignore the minority; when the student leaders met Li Peng on 18 May, Wuer Kaixi told the premier that even 'if one student refuses to leave (the Square) and continues the hunger strike, it will be extremely difficult for us to guarantee that the others will go'. What kind of democracy were they practicing in which the decisions of the elected leaders were not binding on all the students?

Towards the end of the student movement, Wang Dan, a twenty-year-old student from Beijing University and one of the more sophisticated of the leaders, told a reporter that the student demands had 'no framework'. 'I think,' said Wang, 'the student movements in the future should be firmly based on something solid, such as the democratization of campus life or the realization of civil rights according to the Constitution. Otherwise (and he was no doubt reflecting on what had happened in the Square), the result is chaos.' The students, according to Wang, had tried direct democracy 'where everyone is electing leaders and trying to get involved'. This was impractical, he said, 'because it results in frequent changes of leaders and causes disorder.'

The students did have some quite specific demands (already detailed earlier): the two most important were to get rid of corruption (i.e., abuse of power) and to give freedom to the press (i.e., listen to the people). The frustrated workers and wage earners, troubled by inflation and envious of those who had gotten rich under the new system, joined the students, not for Western-style democracy but for a more just regime. If there was an element of democracy in these demands, it was the unspoken desire that the government should somehow be made answerable to the people.

Second, although the Beijing democracy movement did inspire similar demonstrations in some other cities, the protests outside Beijing were significantly smaller, even in Shanghai which is China's largest city with a population of over 10,000,000. Furthermore, Beijing intellectuals had made practically no attempt to influence citizens in the vast countryside where seventy-five per cent of the Chinese live.

Third, from the very beginning of the crisis, all the leaders had expressed the view that most of the students were well-intentioned and had agreed with the students that some reforms were called for. Li Peng expressed this sentiment even in his nefarious martial law speech: '(These) patriotic students hope to promote democracy and overcome corruption, and this is in line with the goals the party and government have tried to achieve.' What the mass of the students failed to comprehend fully was that the environment which had allowed them to continue to demonstrate was created by an inner party struggle for power and not by the students' action *per se* and that the outcome of their movement would depend on which faction won the power struggle.

With the passage of time the situation had become more and more anomalous. The students lacked a unified organization but expected to be treated as an independent body; they refused to give any permanent status to their leaders and yet wanted them to negotiate with the prime minister on equal terms. By 19 May, when Li Peng met the student leaders, a meaningful dialogue had, in any case, become practically impossible because these were the very students who had been calling for the replacement of Li and other senior party and government leaders. Deng was left with two choices: remove himself and his protégés from power or use force to compel the students to leave Tiananmen Square.

Naturally, Deng chose the latter course. And he did this after having persuaded the Politburo, in a secret meeting on the 23rd, to dismiss Zhao from power.

On the 24th, Li re-introduced censorship by appointing a 'working group' to take charge of the media. The next day, Wan Li (seventy-three years old), the chairman of the National People's Congress (the Chinese legislature) and a pivotal figure in Chinese politics, who had cut short his visit to the United States on the 23rd, threw his support behind Deng. On the same day, president Yang Shangkun (eighty-two years old) ordered troops into Beijing. The hard liners had won the battle for domination over the party and the propaganda organs and gained the support of the military.

On the evening of the 25th, television viewers saw a relaxed Li Peng receiving three new foreign ambassadors to China. Li told the emissaries that 'the Chinese government is stable and capable of fulfilling its responsibilities and of properly dealing with the current problems'. He talked of martial law and explained why the troops had not reached the downtown area: 'Anyone with common sense can see that this is not because the troops are unable to enter the downtown area but because the government is the people's government and the People's Liberation Army is the people's own army.' The troops, according to Li, had exercised great restraint because the people had not yet fully grasped the political significance of the 'rebellion' and, therefore, of the need for martial law.

Li also added a note of caution for the outside world: 'What is happening now is China's internal affair. Foreign countries . . . must not interfere in current events.'

The protesters in touch with Zhao's faction knew that the end was in sight, but they had no control over the excited and enthusiastic students in the Square, many of whom had just arrived from colleges and universities in distant cities. On the 27th, Wuer Kaixi and some other leaders, proposed a strategic retreat on the grounds that the sanitary conditions in the Square had deteriorated and posed a health hazard. But few listened to them.

For the next few days an uneasy calm lay over the capital. Parades continued, but they had become commonplace and lost their newsworthiness. They were not reported by the Chinese media, and the foreign press gave them limited space. It was the demonstration in Hong Kong on Sunday the 28th, in support of the democracy movement, that caught the attention of the outside world. Some calculate that a million citizens rallied in the British colony. This, naturally, introduced another element of urgency in the situation because the Chinese leaders, anticipating the return of the colony to China in 1997, were afraid of the consequences of a democracy movement in Hong Kong. 'There is no way for us to retreat,' said president Yang. 'To retreat means our downfall. To retreat means the downfall of the People's Republic of China and the restoration of capitalism.' (This statement must have worried many in Hong Kong.)

On the 30th, the students once again did the unexpected and presented China and the world with an exquisite symbol of their movement: a twenty-seven-foot-high 'Goddess of Democracy', which obviously had been modelled on the American Statue of Liberty. The snow-white goddess, made of Styrofoam and plaster by Beijing art students, was raised directly between the portrait of Mao Zedong, hanging over Tiananmen and the stele honouring the revolutionary martyrs (the Monument to the People's Heroes). In the eyes of the leaders the statue confirmed the 'counterrevolutionary' nature of the movement. Were not the students, in demanding the dismissal of Deng Xiaoping and Li Peng, exhorting the country to overthrow the communist leaders, and did not the statue symbolize their call that China reject socialism and adopt the Western-style bourgeois democratic system? The students compounded their 'guilt' by trying to win foreign TV audiences with placards such as, 'Of the people, by the people, for the people', written in English.

A national television announcer reflected the official position: 'The erection of a so-called statue of a goddess is an insult to our national dignity and mocks our nation's image.' The announcer reported that an angered patriotic citizen had urged that the statue be removed to 'protect the souls of children from unwholesome (i.e., American capitalist) influences.' A Beijing daily condemned the statue for being a symbol of America and admonished the students not to 'poke fun at China's patriotic feelings'. The government tried to counter the student move by organizing 'anti-democracy' demonstrations in which Uncle Sam was shown giving dollars to Fang Lizhi (who had kept aloof from the student movement but was supposed to be one of the brains behind it); an effigy of Fang was later burned. These demonstrations were televised and provided an unmistakable indication that the government saw a 'foreign hand' in the 'conspiracy'. At the same time, government banners carrying such slogans as 'Oppose bourgeois liberalization with a clear-cut stand' and 'Maintain unity and stability' were draped outside some of the major hotels and buildings in the downtown area.

Late on the night of 2 June, 2,000 soldiers in three columns marched towards Tiananmen Square from the east, west and north. The soldiers were very young and inexperienced and not in uniform (they wore white shirts with their army trousers), and they carried no arms, though trucks following them at a discreet distance carried some assault rifles. This 'children's invasion', as one Western reporter dubbed it, was swiftly halted by Beijing residents who had been aroused from their sleep by the students' motorcycle squad that screeched down the roads shouting, 'Troops! Troops!' The troops, bewildered, confused, and humiliated were pushed back, some of the trucks were overturned, the tyres of others were slashed, and a few weapons were 'captured' as trophies.

If the intention of the government was to create a 'serious incident', it had done an admirable job. The government now *had* to recapture the guns and supplies that had fallen into the hands of the 'rebels'. The situation also provided an opportunity to workers, who had formed the illegal 'Federation of Autonomous Workers' Unions', and unemployed citizens to show some muscle. A foreign observer noted that during the daylight hours of 3 June, when the troops for the first time made a stand and used tear gas, truncheons and belts to disperse the throngs, 'the crowd contained fewer students and more workers, fewer teenagers and more tough-looking adults'. Many carried metal pipes, wooden stakes and rocks with which they attacked the troops.

According to a later government report, which may be exaggerated but sounds plausible, the illegal students' unions and the illegal workers' unions distributed 'knives, iron bars, chains and sharpened bamboo sticks', with the exhortation that they should be used to kill the soldiers and members of the security police. The workers also provided instructions 'on how to make and use Molotov cocktails and how to wreck and burn military vehicles'. During the day, mobs did attack the buildings which housed the Party Propaganda Department and the Ministry of Radio, Film and Television, and the entry gates of Zhongnanhai; and they did burn trolley cars and yank out the metal railings, used as road dividers, to block roads and set up barricades.

From the government leaders' point of view, the stage was being set for a 'violent rebellion in an attempt to overthrow the government and seize power at (*sic*) one stroke'. Although the leaders, no doubt, were magnifying the situation, conditions were reaching a critical point. An astute American journalist, Fred Shapiro, a long-time resident of Beijing, observes: 'I was not the only resident on the streets . . . (on the 3rd) who began to feel that the student democracy movement might yet topple the national government leaders.'*

At 6.30 p.m. on the evening of 3 June, an announcement was repeatedly made on television and radio that, 'All citizens must heighten their vigilance and keep off the streets and not go to Tiananmen Square as of the issuing of this notice . . . ; citizens must remain at home to ensure their security.' Another announcement warned that, 'PLA troops must carry out the martial law tasks as planned, and none should prevent them.' As with the earlier martial law edicts, no one seemed to care much about these either.

At 10 p.m., convoys of armoured personnel carriers and tanks carrying regular soldiers (as against the kids sent on the 2nd) armed with AK-47 automatic rifles began to move into the city. It was not easy going. The crowds and barricades slowed down the convoys and gave ample opportunity for the mobs to attack the vehicles with metal clubs and stones, Molotov cocktails and burning blankets. Hundreds of armoured personnel carriers and trucks were destroyed. Several soldiers, not allowed to leave the burning vehicles were incinerated, some were beaten to death, and a few were hanged, doused with gasoline and burned. The soldiers responded with tear gas and bullets. The blood bath had begun.

The final tragic round took place between the midnight of 3 June and

* See 'Letter from Beijing', *The New Yorker*, 19 June 1989

the early dawn hours of 4 June. By 1.30 a.m., on the morning of the 4th, the troops had finally battled their bloody way to Tiananmen Square and surrounded it. Since the troops had been compelled to shoot randomly into the crowds to get them out of their path, there was no way to ensure that some innocent bystanders would not be injured.

Government loudspeakers at the Square then made the following announcement: 'A serious counterrevolutionary rebellion occurred in the capital this evening. Rioters furiously attacked soldiers and robbed them of their weapons and ammunition, burned military vehicles, set up roadblocks and kidnapped officers and men in an effort to subvert the socialist system. The People's Liberation Army has kept an attitude of restraint for some days. However, the counterrevolutionary rebellion must now be resolutely counterattacked. All citizens and students should leave the Square immediately to ensure that martial law troops will be able to implement their task.'

At 4.30 a.m., the loudspeakers broadcast a new notice: 'It is time to leave the Square and the martial law headquarters accepts the request of the students to be allowed to withdraw.' The students filed out of the Square. By 5.30, the tanks had rolled over the tent city and demolished the 'Goddess of Democracy'.

At 7.30 a.m., 4 June, the regime announced that the 'rebellion has been suppressed'.

The Aftermath

Return to Normalcy

In a country where the press, television, and radio are government controlled, and where the decision-making process is hidden from public view, rumours are bound to spread. Though the 'counterrevolutionary rebellion' had been officially suppressed and the attention of the Chinese media had turned to the brave soldiers who had given their lives to save the country from chaos, the mopping up operations continued for another few days and sporadic shooting by the troops in the city resulted in many more unreported deaths. Beijingers talked of thousands killed and of dead bodies shovelled into a mass grave outside the city. Foreign reports mentioned figures ranging from 500 to 3,000 dead. The Voice of America and the BBC news bulletins were listened to avidly and believed as being more truthful than the Chinese media, but the foreign services could do no more than relay the rumours picked up by their reporters in Beijing.

For example, reliable newspapers, such as the *New York Times*, published reports of rumours that Deng had passed away; that Li Peng had been assassinated; that army officers had been executed and army generals were being arrested in various parts of China for refusing to participate in the nationwide crackdown on dissidents. These rumours were credible because none of China's leaders had been seen or heard from for two weeks or more. On 6 June, the outside world was discussing the possibilities of a civil war in China because, to quote the *New York Times*, 'Chinese troops (in Beijing) took up what seemed to be defensive positions . . . that suggested that they feared attacks from other army units (who had refused to move against student demonstrators), and there were reports that clashes between units had already occurred on the outskirts of the capital.' Officials in Washington confirmed these reports, and several American 'China experts' talked of the Chinese officers being 'infected by the democracy movement'. The rumours, which took time to be dispelled, had serious consequences. Foreign students and scholars began to leave China, foreign scholars scheduled to visit China for conferences or research cancelled their trips, and many foreign embassies in Beijing ordered non-essential staff to return home. Washington began to make preparations for a possible military evacuation of Americans in Beijing.

Rumours of a continuing power struggle and civil war were finally laid to rest by the television appearance of Li Peng on 8 June, and of Deng Xiaoping the following day. Li Peng, who made his first appearance after having withdrawn from the public scene for two weeks, praised the troops for their 'fine effort to safeguard the security of the capital' and called on the leaders of the illegal students' union and workers' union to surrender themselves or 'face severe punishment'. On the 9th, the TV covered a meeting of the Central Military Commission and showed the smiling face of the Supreme Leader, Deng Xiaoping, who had not been seen in public for three weeks and had been rumoured to be dead. Deng was surrounded by Li Peng, President Yang, Qiao Shi (head of the Public Security), party veterans such as Li Xiannin (eighty), Peng Zhen (eighty-seven), Bo Yibo (eighty-one), Wan Li (seventy-three) and fifty generals. Deng commended the army for crushing the rebellion and expressed 'heartfelt condolences' for the soldiers and police who had died or been wounded in the 'struggle'. He made no mention of the civilians who had been killed by the soldiers.

Deng Xiaoping's 9 June Speech

In his speech, Deng explained the origins of the crisis and set the tone of the government's future policies.

Deng blamed the 'turmoil' on the social and intellectual climate created by 'international and domestic' factors, and declared that the 'storm' had arisen 'independent of man's will'. He reiterated that the use of the term 'turmoil' in the 26 April editorial was absolutely correct, and he blamed persons like Zhao Ziyang for having objected to the word. Deng said that China had 'never experienced such a situation before', and that 'a rebellious clique' had confused the innocent and misguided them. '*The key point is that they wanted to overthrow our state and the party .... Their goal was to establish a bourgeois republic entirely dependent on the West* .... (slogans such as combating corruption) were just a front.'

Deng emphasized that the turmoil had been successfully dealt with because 'we still have a *large group of veterans* who have experienced many storms and have a thorough understanding of things'.

Answering the widely-asked question about the use of the PLA in putting down the civil disturbances and its impact on the morale of the armed forces, Deng said that it was 'a severe political test for our army, and the PLA passed muster'.

> The PLA losses were great, but this enabled us to win the support of the people .... (The) PLA is truly a Great Wall of iron and steel of the party and country ...; this army of ours is forever an army under the leadership of the party, forever the defender of the

country, forever the defender of socialism, forever the defender of public interest . . . ; we should never forget how cruel our enemies are. *For them we should not have an iota of forgiveness.*

Deng then turned to the relationship between social unrest and the new economic and political policies. He had 'pondered' over the matter, he said, and come to the conclusion that the strategic goal of economic growth had been a success, and that the policy of (1) making economic development the nation's central task, (2) upholding the four cardinal principles, and (3) persisting in the policy of reform and opening up, were not wrong.

The turmoil did mean that there was a clash between the four cardinal principles and bourgeois liberalization, but,

> The fault does not lie in the four cardinal principles themselves, but in wavering in upholding them, *and in the very poor work done to persist in political work and education* . . . ; and this doesn't apply to schools and students alone, but to the masses as a whole. And we have not said much about plain living and the enterprising spirit, about what kind of country China is and how it is going to turn out. *This is our biggest omission.*

Deng said that in adopting the Open Door policy, China did 'run the risk of importing evil influences from the West', and that he had 'never underestimated such influences'. But,

> In political reforms we can affirm one point: we have to adhere to the system of the National People's Congress and *not the American system of the separation of three powers*. The US berates us for suppressing students. But when they handled domestic student unrest and turmoil, didn't they send out police and troops to arrest people and cause bloodshed? They were suppressing students and the people, but we are putting down a counterrevolutionary rebellion.

Deng concluded with the recommendation that China persist in implementing the basic line already formulated: 'What is important is that we should never change China back into a closed country.'

Later, Deng's speech, because it 'cleared up confused ideas and unified people's thinking', was made a subject of compulsory study for party and government leaders, party members, government employees, teachers and students.

CCP Endorses Deng

On 24 June, the Central Committee of the CCP held a plenary session to endorse Deng's view of the Tiananmen incident. In the communique issued at the end of the meeting the Central Committee, as one would have expected, concluded that 'a very small number of people, taking advantage of student unrest, stirred up a planned, organized and premediated political turmoil in Beijing and some other places, which later developed into a counterrevolutionary rebellion in Beijing'.

The Central Committee praised the contributions made by the 'veteran proletarian revolutionaries, with Deng Xiaoping as their representatives . . . the PLA, the armed police and the public security police'.

The session approved Li Peng's evaluation of Zhao Ziyang's role in the turmoil. Zhao had 'made the mistake of supporting the turmoil and splitting the party and he had unshirkable responsibilities for the development of the turmoil . . . ; he took a passive approach to the four cardinal principles and opposition to bourgeois liberalization, and gravely neglected party building, cultural and ethical development and ideological and political work, causing serious losses to the party'.

Because of these mistakes, Zhao was dismissed from his posts of party general secretary, vice-chairman of the Central Military Commission, membership of the Politburo, and from all other offices in the party. However, he was allowed to retain his party membership.

The session commended Deng's 9 June speech for being a 'programmatic document' which everyone should study; it also admonished the party to enhance ideological education 'in patriotism, socialism, independence and self-reliance, plain living and hard work, and oppose bourgeois liberalization in real earnest'.

In addition to Zhao Ziyang, Hu Qili, a member of the Politburo in charge of overall propaganda work, was also purged.

National People's Congress Endorses Deng

On 29 June, the Standing Committee of the National People's Congress (the body that looks after national affairs between the periodic meetings of the legislature), presided over by Wan Li, met and endorsed the decisions of the Party Central Committee. The Standing Committee of the NPC decided to publish a draft law on demonstrations which stipulated, in Wan Li's words, that 'while exercising their freedom and rights, *citizens must not infringe on the interests of the state, society and collective, or on the legitimate freedom and rights of other citizens*'.

The law stipulated that future organizers of rallies and parades must seek prior permission from the public security departments and must 'make clear their purpose, posters, slogans, the number of participants, hours and places of starting and ending, route, and the names, professions and addresses of the organizers'. No demonstration that undermined 'national unity' was to be permitted, no foreigner could participate in a demonstration by Chinese people without permission (would that mean that foreign journalists would not be allowed to cover the demonstration?), and no rally could be held within a certain distance of important state organs (this ruled out demonstrations in Tiananmen Square in the future), military installations, airports, etc., or near foreign diplomatic missions.

Authorized View of the Spring Revolt

During the session of the Standing Committee of the NPC, Chen Xitong, the mayor of Beijing, presented a detailed (and, no doubt, officially approved) analysis of the 'counterrevolutionary rebellion'. He reported that the turmoil was a premeditated 'political conspiracy' hatched by 'a tiny handful of people *both inside and outside the party*', who had propagated bourgeois liberalization by 'echoing the strategy of Western countries'. The conspirators had made 'organizational preparations for years' and '*colluded with foreign forces*' to spread their ideology and foster a counterrevolutionary public opinion. Referring to the 'foreign hand', he said:

> Some political forces in the West have always attempted to make the socialist countries, including China, give up the socialist road, eventually bringing these countries under the rule of international capital and put(ting) them on the course of capitalism.

Mayor Chen traced the source of the troubles within the party to events in September 1988, when Zhao Ziyang and his 'brains trust' used the Hong Kong press to mount a campaign promoting the idea that Deng (whom they derogatively referred to as 'the super old man') should be replaced by Zhao. Chen then revealed how Zhao's group had worked closely with intellectuals, like Professor Fang Lizhi, who had been dismissed from the party for their anti-party activities. Chen gave names and details that provide a fascinating insight into the nature of the liberal opposition that was developing in the country.

According to Chen, Zhao Ziyang had helped the 'democracy virus' to spread to the campuses, where 'big and small character posters', attacking the party and the socialist system and the person of Deng Xiaoping, began to appear in increasing numbers. Chen portrayed Fang Lizhi as a truly evil figure who called for total Westernization and propagated the notion that socialism had 'completely lost its attraction'. Chen disclosed that Fang's wife, Li Shuxian, was also involved in the conspiracy.

Chen Xitong then recounted, step-by-step, the development of the student movement, how it was exploited by the 'tiny handful' of conspirators, how Zhao Ziyang's 4 May speech was 'diametrically opposed' to the spirit of the 26 April editorial which had been endorsed by Deng and the Politburo, and how this speech marked the escalation of the confrontation between the counterrevolutionaries and the government.

After analyzing the conditions that had made it imperative that martial law be imposed, Chen concluded by describing the brutality with which the soldiers had been treated by the 'counterrevolutionaries'. According to Chen, over 6,000 martial law soldiers and security police were injured, and the death toll 'reached several dozens'; 1,280 military and other vehicles, including sixty armoured personnel carriers, were wrecked; and over 3,000 civilians were wounded 'and over 200, including thirty-six college students died during the riot'. These facts, said Chen, went counter to the rumours of 'thousands of people massacred', and of the 'Tiananmen Square bloodbath'—rumours that had been '*spread by the Voice of America and some people who deliberately wished to spread rumours*'.

The hard liners were now fully entrenched. They had explained the sinister nature of the turmoil, identified their enemies, got rid of the most important person opposing them (which prepared the way for widespread dismissals of Zhao Ziyang's followers), and lined up the party and the propaganda machine behind them. The official myth now promoted was that the so-called 'massacre' was a figment of Western imagination and that what actually took place was largely a public-supported peaceful operation against a 'small number of bad elements'. Television, radio, newspapers, and magazines were flooded with photographs (secretly taken by hidden government cameras) of 'conspirators' talking to foreigners, of soldiers being beaten up, and of patriotic families handing over 'wanted criminals' to the police. The media also presented reports of how the 'good', common citizens had helped the soldiers in their hour of need, and it gave eyewitness accounts of how thugs and counter-revolutionaries, aided by the foreign press and TV, had spread false rumours of indiscriminate killings, and so on. History was being revised in haste.

Those who know China were not surprised at the quickness with which calm was restored and life returned to normal. This had much to do with the traditional docility of the population and its acceptance of strong authority; in communist China it was only when authority was split and did not speak with one voice that dissidents got an opportunity to surface. And whenever this has happened, a strong leadership, that considered flexibility a sign of weakness, has re-exerted itself aggressively; the dissidents have usually been declared to be 'counterrevolutionary' and state violence has been used unhesitatingly to put them down.

The return of apparent calm after the June Massacre does not, however, mean that the problems that led to the trouble have been resolved. The reimposition of harsher, more authoritarian policies will only be able to stem, not reverse, the trend towards a more open political system.

Foreign Reaction

Foreign reaction was instant and widespread. The world condemned the massacre, though official comments in countries friendly to Beijing (mostly Afro-Asian), or wanting to win the favour of Beijing (like India and the USSR), were muted. The strongest disapproval came from West Europe and the United States, though Eastern Europe also expressed some shock. Foreign commentators talked of China's brutal suppression of peaceful demonstrators, the butchery of unarmed citizens, the rise of Stalinist terror in China, and of the return to power of aged conservative revolutionaries whose death (in the not too distant future) might lead the country into chaos. The official Hungarian paper wrote that, 'Our own history has taught us that truth does not come out of a gun barrel, and neither do solutions.'

China protested the official comments by Western governments as an 'interference in China's internal affairs' and advised foreign powers to refrain from such activity 'in the interest of friendly relations'.

Of all the countries, China was most worried about reactions in the United States. America had developed very special relations with China, and Beijing needed the goodwill of the Americans in its efforts to modernize. The US was a key source for industrial and military technology and for investment capital; China had a huge number of joint enterprises with Americans which brought hard currency; the bulk of the foreign tourists (not including overseas Chinese) came from America; and not least important, there were 40,000 Chinese students still in American educational institutions and a large number of American specialists training the Chinese in China itself.

The violent suppression of human rights during the democracy movement, followed by the arrest and execution of 'counterrevolutionaries', repelled the public in the US, and Sino–US relations were strained. Though the State Department, not wanting to impair the 'strategic' value of China to US geo-political interests (the US did not want to drive China into the arms of Russia) was anxious not to go too far in its criticism of the Chinese government, public opinion made it necessary that president Bush take some measures against Beijing. The administration halted military sales to

China, banned high-level diplomatic and military exchanges and pushed to freeze all bank loans to China from the International Monetary Fund and the World Bank; it also made it easier for Chinese students in America to gain extensions on their visas. The US Congress called for tougher sanctions but, by and large, the United States' moves were cautiously limited.

Although the US action, coupled with similar action by other Western nations and Japan (such as the suspension of official and multilateral loans, and the slowdown of trade and investment) did hurt Beijing's development plans, the desire for profits brought most of the capitalists scurrying back to a China in which 'order' had been restored so rapidly. By August even the families of the diplomats were returning to Beijing.

One irritant in Chinese–American relations was the granting of protection to Fang Lizhi and his wife in the US embassy in Beijing. The Chinese, who had dubbed Fang 'a traitor and a counterrevolutionary', had issued a warrant for his arrest and wanted the embassy to hand him over to the Chinese authorities. Later, however, in an attempt to mollify Western opinion Fang was allowed to leave for England where he will work at Cambridge University.

To sum up, the student demonstrations in Beijing, which began in mid-April 1989 and were crushed so ruthlessly six weeks later, on 4 June, came to be dubbed, variously, as 'a democracy movement', 'a civil rights movement', 'a people's power movement', 'a historic upheaval' and 'a revolution'. These appellations, devised by one segment or the other of an ill-organized student body at various stages of the Spring Revolt, cannot be taken too literally, though many foreign journalists, attempting to provide an instant understanding of Chinese politics, did exactly that. In the beginning the student demands were simple and limited. Indeed, they accorded with the declared policies of the government: the students called for the eradication of corruption, more funds for education, better treatment of intellectuals, and the hastening of the democratic process. Most important, they wanted to open a dialogue with the leaders. The initial inflexibility with which the party responded to the student demands resulted in the enlargement of the arena of protest and an open defiance of governmental authority by the students. When the leadership softened its stand, the students, believing that they had 'defeated' the government, made their demands harsher, and compromise became difficult.

Unfortunately, the split between the Conservatives and the Reformers over the stand to be taken, led to policy shifts between a hard and a soft line. In the final round the hard liners took over, imposed martial law, and when the students refused to obey the martial law regulations, the authorities used guns and tanks to crush the 'counterrevolutionary rebellion'.

International television networks, with their capacity to present graphic, eye-rivetting pictures of the drama as it unfolded, and the TV commentators' yearning to report the 'making of history', oversimplified the complex political situation; many of these commentators displayed a colossal lack of appreciation for China's unique tradition and process of modernization, both of which have played a critical role in the shaping of the demonstrations and their suppression. The situation, no doubt, was aggravated by the fact that, in spite of Deng Xiaoping's Open Door policy, the decision-making process in China remains carefully hidden, not only from foreigners but also the Chinese. The eighty-five-year-old Deng Xiaoping, the Supreme Leader, continues to wield extraordinary power, although he holds no official post.

The Spring disturbance, which nearly destroyed the credibility of the communist party leadership and Deng Xiaoping's reform programme, was not a discrete political event. It was a part of the ongoing conflict between the Chinese Communist Party and the Chinese intelligentsia, each side representing a different view of modernization, and its origins can be traced to the war years (1937–45), when Mao Zedong first established himself as the absolute leader of the party and enunciated his ideology. Furthermore, since the intelligentsia is located both outside and inside the party, this conflict has been reflected not only in the relations between the CCP and the citizenry, but also in inner party discords and strife.

Conclusion

In the 1990s the communist world is passing through changes of monumental historical significance. Spontaneous popular unrest is forcing the hard line communist governments in the Eastern Bloc to voluntarily give up power and democratize politics. Never has the ideal of Western liberal democracy appeared more attractive than it does today. Only time will tell whether this passionate call for democracy presages the death of communist ideology, or if it only marks a temporary disarray of the socialist system. However, it is striking that China seems to remain unaffected, at least outwardly, by these forces of change.

Interestingly enough, it was China under Deng that was the first among the communist nations to challenge the rigidity of Marxist thought and move towards a Western-style market-oriented economy! And the Chinese economic reform programmes did result in the emergence of radical ideas that called for a change in the socialist system, but the tanks at Tiananmen Square crushed all hopes, at least for some time to come, for the realization of what was pejoratively termed 'bourgeois liberalization'. Today, Chinese leaders are reinforcing the role of the communist party while at the same time endeavouring to maintain the drive towards economic liberalization; the Europeans, on the other hand, are liberalizing politics because they consider that to be a precondition for economic reforms.

The reason China has remained untouched so far by the storm in Europe is to be found in China's unique socio-political environment. The Eastern Bloc countries are far more industrialized than China, their working classes are literate and have a strong sense of solidarity, and their intelligentsia is not isolated from the masses. To take two examples from Europe: in Poland the democracy movement has been worker-led but fully supported by the intelligentsia; in Czechoslovakia the movement has been led by the students and the intelligentsia, but has the solid backing of the working classes. In contrast to Eastern Europe, the Beijing-led dissident movement was neither mass-based nor widespread. In China the dissident students and the dissident intellectuals are not only alienated from the largely illiterate working classes (seventy-five per cent of whom are peasants and quite divorced from the urban-based intelligentsia), but do not even command the full support of the nation's intelligentsia.

The Chinese intellectuals are not unified by any cohesive set of ideas. Indeed, they are split into mutually antagonistic groups, each one reflecting the views of its patron in the party, who might be a Reformer like Hu Yaobang or a Conservative like Chen Yun. The incapacity of the Chinese intelligentsia to dislodge the leadership is, therefore, wholly understandable. It is also understandable why the ruthless suppression of the immature, naïve, dissident youth in Beijing did not result in any widespread turmoil. The youth had neither sought, nor received, the support of the peasantry and in the national context, the number of workers in Beijing, Shanghai, and the other cities, who joined the demonstrators was relatively small. At the height of the movement, most of the older and more respected intellectuals (the great Fang Lizhi included) kept away from the demonstrations and made no public expression of their support or sympathy.

It is also relevant to mention the role of the church in the Eastern Bloc. Throughout the period of communist ascendancy in Europe, the church, however harshly suppressed, remained an active symbol of opposition and a focal point of popular loyalty. There is no analogous religious institution in China with a similar potential.

However, the calm that has returned to the Chinese scene in the aftermath of the Tiananmen Square Incident is misleading, and the Chinese leaders still face a crisis. The social-economic-political picture in China is becoming exceedingly confused, and the alarming gaps between the party's ideological pronouncements and the Chinese reality are widening. Deng's oft-repeated guidelines, that exhort the party and the people to simultaneously uphold the Four Principles and follow the course of reform and opening to the outside world, are self-contradictory and offer no unity of thought and action. Indeed, the reforms have created political problems and social disparities that are inherently explosive in nature and cannot be contained within the parameters of the Four Principles. Deng should be aware of this. During his years of supreme command, he himself has done no more than shift his support back and forth between the right and the left, hoping all the while that somehow

China will achieve his vision of a prosperous society without losing its socialist discipline and values. That he has had to jettison both his chosen successors, Hu Yaobang and Zhao Ziyang, should have revealed the gravity of the predicament, but, surprisingly, Deng remains optimistic.

According to Deng, the party must persist in maintaining strong centralized control over the country but withdraw from interfering directly in the operation of government enterprises. In practice, this is an impossible task. Wherever the party's monopoly of power has been reduced, for example, in the collective and private enterprises, the party has come to be considered redundant and has lost prestige.

There are, perhaps, two possible ways that the party can carry out a devolution of its power and yet retain its leadership. One way is for China to establish a strong legal system and procedures for democratic decision-making and democratic supervision; in other words, some kind of system of checks backed by laws. Jiang Zemin, speaking at a rally in September 1989, declared this to be the goal of the party, hastening to add that the 'building of democracy and a legal system still remain an extremely arduous task'. In a similar statement, Deng, too, while maintaining that 'democracy is an important means of carrying out our reforms', went on to explain that it was impossible to 'put it into practice':

> China is such a huge country, with such an enormous population, so many nationalities and such varied conditions that it is not yet possible to hold direct elections at higher levels. Furthermore, the people's education level is too low. So we have to stick to the system of people's congresses, in which democratic centralism is applied. The Western two-chamber, multi-party system won't work in China. China also has a number of democratic parties, but they all accept the leadership of the Communist Party. Ours is a system under which we (who is the we?) make decisions after consultation with all other parties. *In this connection, even Westerners* (one wonders which Westerners he had in mind!) *agree that in a country as vast as China, if there were no central leadership many problems would be hard to solve*—first of all, the problem of food. Our reform cannot depart from socialism, it

cannot be accomplished without the leadership of the Communist Party . . . .

(Our) present structure of leadership has some advantages. For example, it enables us to make quick decisions, while if we place too much emphasis on a need for checks and balances, problems may arise.

Since Deng appears to be convinced that there is no alternative to the present system it comes as no surprise that all attempts by the party to reform the political structure have so far failed to produce any significant results.

The other way that the leadership can possibly resolve the dilemma, a route which Deng would favour, is for the party to take the nebulous notion of what Deng calls 'socialism with Chinese characteristics' and work it into a cohesive, well-defined ideology—an ideology which would inspire the nation to employ and exploit capitalistic devices to modernize the economy and also instil in the people a hatred for the liberal pluralism that characterizes Western-style representative democracy. Since the likelihood of such a novel, self-contradictory ideology ever emerging is difficult to imagine, the party most likely will become even more authoritarian and find its legitimacy in its power to use brutal, arbitrary, and dictatorial methods of control.

The situation today is that the party has no ideology worth talking about; it is rent by bickering factions and does not even present a unified facade to the people. After every popular upheaval, Deng has tried to bring back party discipline and force party members to live up to the values of austerity, altruism, and self-sacrifice. The irony is that he has not been able to achieve this goal through ideological education and has had to force party members to be 'honest' and 'virtuous' by threats of punishment. Thus in 1988, 20,000 party members were expelled and another 89,000 asked to resign because of corrupt practices. A similar purge took place in 1989. However, these actions have failed to intimidate the bulk of the forty-nine million party members, who continue to believe that they cannot be denied the right to get rich along with the rest of the nation. If it ever comes to pass that party members are denied this right, no talented and ambitious young person would be attracted to apply for party membership and, thereby, destroy his, or her, options for upward mobility.

Perhaps the least that the party can do is to strengthen its own organization by making 'democratic centralism' a matter of fact rather than an empty slogan. But here, too, the impact of Deng and Mao has had a negative repercussion. These two Supreme Leaders never allowed party rules and regulations to come in the way of their schemes. When Hu Yaobang was dismissed, Deng called an enlarged meeting of the Politburo (though not permitted to do so under the rules of the party constitution), packed the meeting with his friends and cronies to gain a majority, and forced Hu to resign. Zhao Ziyang's departure from power was 'legalized' after the event. And as for the decision to use the military on 4 June, Deng went outside the party centre and mustered the backing of the 'large group of veterans who have experienced many storms and have a thorough understanding of things'. Indeed, the 'Gang of the Old', as this group has come to be dubbed, is currently running the show in Beijing.

In November 1989, Deng Xiaoping finally relinquished the office of chairmanship of the Central Military Commission, the last formal post that he held. The post has gone to Jiang Zemin, the current general secretary and Deng's third hand-picked successor. This change does not in any way diminish Deng's national stature or his power to guide China's political process. After stepping down, Deng blessed the new arrangement, saying that his 'mind was (now) very much at ease'. Mao had used practically the same language when he elevated Hua Guofeng to the post of premier, and we know what happened to Hua. This style of personalized authority has kept China from developing mechanisms for a smooth transition of power and weakened national institutions which are needed to provide the framework for growth and modernization. Furthermore, by placing themselves above the party and arbitrating the political process by manipulating one faction against another, Mao and Deng encouraged factionalism that has emasculated the party and given it a bad name.

At this stage, it is difficult to conceive the likelihood of any kind of collective leadership emerging after the death of Deng Xiaoping. The zigzag course of advances and retreats that the party has followed ever since the establishment of the People's Republic is likely to continue to characterize developments for the foreseeable future.

In the confusion created by the Tiananmen Incident several dissident students and intellectuals (included among whom are the student leader Wuer Kaixi and Zhao Ziyang's close advisor Yan Jiaqi) managed to escape from China and find refuge in the West. This group, along with many self-exiled Chinese students (who have decided not to return to China till it becomes more liberal) met in Paris and established a 'Front for Democracy in China' (FDC). Their aim is two-fold: (1) to keep the China issue internationally alive by countering the campaign of disinformation being carried on by the Beijing leaders, and (2) to maintain contacts with like-minded compatriots inside China, and to use various unorthodox channels to disseminate the 'truth' within the country where the media have, once again, come to be gagged.

Although, the FDC lacks funds and its activities are primarily symbolic and pose no real threat to the Chinese government, its members are optimistic about the future of democracy in their motherland. They believe that both external and internal conditions are currently working in their favour and rapidly undermining the power of the 'Gang of the Old' to suppress popular opposition. Their argument is that external pressures, stemming from the rapid changes taking place in the Eastern Bloc and the Soviet Union, are bound to have an impact on China. They assert that, sooner or later, the Soviet Communist Party, too, will lose its monopoly of power, and they ask: when that happens, will the Chinese Communist Party be able to hold on to its claim that 'China is different', that 'China has its own standard of human rights', that patriotism in China is faith in the socialist path and leadership of the CCP, and that only the CCP can lead the country into modernity?

Internally, according to the members of the FDC, Deng Xiaoping's desperate attempt to win the hearts and minds of the populace, by re-introducing Maoist-style ideological mass campaigns, is doomed to failure because the Deng group has lost its moral authority to rule the country; the disillusioned Chinese people can no longer be manipulated by hollow slogans. And that, in any case, the party which, itself, is ideologically bankrupt and lacks a sense of unity and discipline cannot be expected to set an example to the people. Matters have been made worse by the economic retrenchment programmes: the closing down of many of the profit-making private and collective enterprises has resulted in millions losing their jobs and, as a consequence, their faith in the party.

The FDC members relish the predicament in which Deng finds himself, caught as he is between the desire to uphold his liberalizing economic reform programmes and the compulsion to revive the old, centralized command techniques of economic control. The dissidents conclude that because of this dilemma the policies of the Chinese leaders are bound to remain confused and can only help in aggravating the growing problems connected with the country's internal and external debt, lack of balance between agricultural and industrial growth, economic shortages, inflation, unfair distribution of social wealth, and corruption.

The dissidents are also hopeful that Deng's Open Door policy will help their cause because it has put the party in a quandary: the party can neither close the door to the outside world, which it absolutely must if it wants to re-exert Maoist-style controls over the population; nor can it keep the door open because that will, inevitably, allow 'evil' liberalizing influences to creep into the country. The party's attempts to close the door half-way by cutting down on contacts with foreigners and other nations (for example, by making it difficult for students to go abroad) are bound to undermine the modernization programme and prove self-defeating.

As the first anniversary of the 4 June Tiananmen Square Massacre came and went, fears of another massacre of the innocents went unfounded as Deng's government kept a close watch on dissident activity and took unprecedented security measures to ensure that there were no demonstrations. But stability is still only an illusion in China today and all a divided leadership has been able to do is attempt to stifle dissent on the one hand while trying to put the best face on an unpopular regime on the other (recent measures to achieve the latter objective have included decisions to relax the government's two-year-old economic austerity programme, lift martial law in Beijing and Lhasa and tone down the ideological hard line). In sum, the complex issues of democracy and social justice are not in any way nearer resolution. A long-time Asian diplomat in China has summed up the situation very neatly: 'The present dispensation will stay: it is not as transitory as Chinese dissidents and Westerners wish, nor is it as stable and united as the Beijing authorities make out. The poor intellectuals can continue to agonize.'